BLINDSIDED

finding joy through tragedy

BY MICHAEL BARNES

First edition published
August, 2014

For information regarding bulk purchases of this book, digital
purchase and special discounts, please contact the Author.

Manufactured in the United States of America
ISBN 978-0-9905630-0-6

CONTENTS

CONTENTS

DEDICATION

I would like to dedicate this journal to my son Luke and my wife Tracey.

The love I have for my son is what influenced me to write this journal. It is my chance to share with him the journey God took me on to fall in love with Christ. I pray that the words I have written will draw his heart closer to God.

Finally, my sweet wife Tracey has painstakingly shared in much of the writing process. With compassion and patience she has allowed me to reflect back on my journey while bringing forward many of the wounds that will always be a part of me. She has offered me her shoulder to cry on when the writing process opened wounds, and comforted me as I went through the process of putting them into a story with the hope that I could help others. She has patiently listened to my story time and time again, guiding some of the writing with suggestions for improved readability and clarity.

The completion of this journal was a direct result of my love for my wife, my son, and Christ. Tracey, I love you. May the journey we continue to share together be one that draws us both into the hands and heart of God.

ACKNOWLEDGEMENTS

One of the first things I learned when life humbled me, was how much I needed my community of family, friends, clients and co-workers. I have always found it difficult to ask for help when I am struggling. My pride stands tall, unwilling to give way and prevents my community of loved ones from serving me when I need them the most.

Being a follower of Christ, I do understand the internal blessing you feel when you help someone in need. It truly is an opportunity to bring glory to God when your heart is open to serve; you feel God nudge you, you follow the lead of the Holy Spirit, and then watch God work His miracles. Sometimes it's hard to tell who is blessed more, you...or the person you've helped. Understanding this, I knew when my wife left that I needed to allow my community of loved ones to help me through this trial. I knew allowing them to help me was not only blessing me, but was also an opportunity for them to be blessed by God.

It is with the deepest gratitude that I have an opportunity to acknowledge my community of loved ones that stood in the gap for my son and me and helped us both manage an extremely challenging circumstance in our lives. You helped us move forward providing emotional, spiritual and financial support. I truly cannot thank you enough for the godly example you showed to my son and to me.

Unfortunately, I do not have enough space to thank everyone who helped me and my son, but I would like to thank these individuals personally for your help and support: my business partner Jon Black for taking a great deal of the burden of running our business as I adjusted to the difficulties of the separation. My clients Tam and Norma de St. Aubin, Maureen and Meredith Barkley, and Seymour Levin for the financial support they provided me as I adjusted to surviving on a single income. There is also one more couple who has requested to remain anonymous but the story of the financial assistance they provided me is included in this journal. Thank you for giving me an opportunity to see faith in action.

I would like to thank my mother, Marti Davis for her love and emotional support as well as showing up at my house every Monday morning at 5:30 AM so I could continue to work and provide income for my son.

I was also given specific advice regarding how to deal with the emotional wounds of divorce for my son from Kathryn K. Hatfield. I am very thankful for the advice, support, and guidance she provided me and my former wife that helped us to minimize the initial emotional wounds of the separation for him. She played a vital role in the healing process for us all and I will always hold her close to my heart.

My heartfelt thanks go to these individuals for a number of different reasons: Beth Anderson, John and Ruth Harris, Art and Shelley Fadde, Gene and Linda Matin as well as my entire Divorce Care classmates, the Divorce Care program, my entire personal training staff at DownTown Fitness on Elm, and all my clients and friends. I can't thank you enough for being a part of God's plan to bring healing and reconciliation to my heart.

I think it is important to understand how difficult it was for me to share such a personal life experience. This was one of the most challenging parts of my journey because I did not want to emotionally hurt my former wife. I knew that sharing our story would expose parts of our life that could place her in the vulnerable position of being judged. All I can say is--it takes two for a marriage to work and two for a marriage to fail. Therefore, I would like to thank my former wife for allowing me to share such a personal part of our life with the hope that it will point other hearts toward reconciliation and help spare the fragile hearts of children who are often hurt by separation and divorce.

Finally, there are a number of contributors to this journal I would like to thank personally for your ideas and editing during the writing process. My father Charles Barnes, John d'Elia, Anne Osborne, Janet Ward Black, Chris Lewis, Kathy Sohn, Don Miller, Gerard Davidson, my father-in-law Steve Gallop, GT Freeman, Jeff Jones, my former brother-in-law Alex Shelton, my publishing consultant Mike Simpson, and my wonderful wife Tracey Shrouder. Your contributions have helped an inexperienced writer share this personal journey with the hope that it will help others find and experience the healing power and forgiveness found in Christ.

THE PREFACE

This forty-day journal was written as God took me on a journey to find myself after I had been blindsided by the loss of my marriage. My journey began with me lying on the floor crying out to God in agony, but by His mercy I was lifted out of the pit of despair. God picked me up by the miracle of the Holy Spirit He put in me. As my pride fell away, I began to see with clarity the wisdom of God's love story found in my Savior Jesus. As I surrendered to the Holy Spirit, I experienced my first real relationship with Jesus. The words in this journal reflect my personal journey to find and experience the love of Christ inside me. It is my hope that my story helps bring healing and reconciliation to you.

> **Psalm 40:1-3** I waited patiently for the Lord; he turned to me and heard my cry. He lifted me out of the slimy pit, out of the mud and mire; he set my feet on a rock and gave me a firm place to stand. He put a new song in my mouth, a hymn of praise to our God. Many will see and fear the Lord and put their trust in him.

I pray that the words written in this journal will point your heart toward the healing power of Jesus. I pray that out of your struggle and your suffering, you will find peace and experience the love of God found in the Holy Spirit. As His love heals your wounds, I pray that you will experience the joy and miracle of this amazing gift that lives in you. Finally, I pray that you will see that sharing His love and forgiveness with others is part of His plan to bring the healing power of Jesus alive and into this broken world.

PART ONE

My Story: Finding Joy through Tragedy

1

The Preparation

What happens when someone you love dearly hurts you so deeply just breathing seems impossible? What happens when the pain from betrayal makes everything inside you want to lash out in anger? What words can possibly make sense when these terrible wounds cause us so much pain?

Why, God? Why would You let this happen to me? Why would You take apart something I thought You had put together? Why do You let horrible things happen to people who love You? Why, God, why? Where are You in all of this, Lord? All I wanted was to be a good man and trust You, and this is what I get in return? Why do You let this world You created cause so much pain and sorrow?

What if the answer to all these questions was: "My child, I just want you to be closer to Me."?

This forty-day journal was written as I struggled with those agonizing questions when my wife of eleven and a half years walked away from our marriage for a co-worker. I was wallowing in a heap of self-pity, wondering why God would allow this to happen to me. I thought I was a good husband, a good provider for my family, and a good father to my four-year-old son. This just didn't seem to make any sense.

Ten years prior to this life-altering event, I had given my heart to Jesus and slowly started to give control of my life over to God. He continually proved trustworthy through each major life event when I put my trust in Him, and things always seemed to work out. These were the times God drew me closer, but where was He now? Often I could see His wisdom in my circumstances, but not now! We hear so often that suffering is part of the Christian walk, but it had not been mine—not real pain and real heartache. It was surreal; I couldn't believe it really was happening to me. I felt God had betrayed me in this very moment, abandoned me from His protection after a year of events that had softened my pride and allowed me to feel so close to my Maker. What I didn't realize at this moment was that God was preparing me for the journey on which He was about to take me.

I feel that inherent in all of us is the expectation that God will find favor with us as we attempt to align our hearts with His will and obey His Word. Because I declared Jesus to be the Lord of my life, I felt God was going to protect me and my family; however, understanding what God's "protection" means may be one of the great mysteries of Christianity.

It wasn't long after I made my commitment to follow Jesus that I experienced a series of professional trials that started testing my faith. It began when my wife and I sustained a financial loss after we attempted to enter a business partnership with someone who turned out to be incapable of managing money. After it became apparent the business would fail, my wife and I decided it was time to leave. Unfortunately, I knew leaving would cost us a substantial amount of money, because I had used poor judgment and co-signed on a large loan before we finalized our business partnership. Now, I knew when the business failed, that we were going to be responsible for paying off the debt. In addition, I also personally loaned money to this individual when the business was in financial trouble and we would lose that money as well. Despite this, I knew it was time to let go of the money and move forward to purse my own dreams.

Facing the challenges of opening a new business, God proved He was trustworthy. New opportunities opened up allowing my wife and me as well as two new business partners to open a new business in ninety-four days. Due to current changes in lending, we each had to personally guarantee our equipment leases, loans, and building lease. Basically, my business partners and I signed our lives away on a hope and prayer that we could succeed in the same type of business that had failed due to poor financial management.

Using a sound financial plan and offering quality service, it didn't take long for us to reach the top of our industry. As I reflected on my journey, I realized that the trials I had endured were building blocks to establish better money managing skills so I could run a financially sound business. Wisdom sometimes comes only when your heart is prepared and ready to see the picture God is painting for you.

After the initial challenges of starting our own small business, my wife and I embarked on the journey of becoming parents. The journey consisted of a long and trying struggle with infertility. After almost two years of trying to conceive a child and enduring the pain and sorrow of failure, my wife and I experienced the miracle of our son Luke entering the world. Everything in my life completely changed when I held him in my arms. In that moment, something inside me demanded I become a better man, a man worthy of being a father. I started to spend more time praying and reading with a deep desire to show my son the heart of Jesus. Following this new passion, I stumbled across a book by C.S. Lewis called *Mere Christianity*. I drank in his deep Christian philosophy which blew me away. He was an intellectual giant whose arguments solidified my personal faith in Jesus. The book also opened my heart to prepare me for the trial I was about to endure.

To be honest, deep down I continued to struggle with the idea that God was in control of my finances as well as other areas of my life. I built walls of pride, rationalizing why I alone was responsible for managing those parts of my life. I made great arguments to justify my pride and kept God as far from those areas of my life as I possibly could.

At the beginning of 2010, I felt I was missing parts of God's message to me and needed to start trusting all of my life to Him. I spent the first part of the year reading a book by Dave Ramsey called, *Total Money Makeover*. As I read it, it became clear that I needed to move my life toward debt-free living so I could truly be in a position to maximize my giving to God. It was amazing; as my heart changed, I found it more important to maximize my giving rather than my savings. As my personal philosophy about money changed, I felt free. I began making financial changes and restructured our debt to pay off everything over a period of sixteen months. After that, I bought a used car instead of trying to manage a new car payment.

Everything in my life seemed to be coming together. I never felt so close to God, and He was showing me that I could trust Him. I finally started to feel a sense of peace as the year 2010 was coming to an end. My son was getting ready to start kindergarten; my business had survived the financial turmoil of the 2008 collapse along with the sluggish recovery; my marriage seemed to be going well; and my financial future started to look bright. I guess this is what you might call, "the calm before the storm."

I remember sitting at my computer one night about six months before my world crumbled. I was continuing to struggle with giving over control of my financial life to God. While praying, I asked Him to bring whatever storms might be necessary to help me trust Him to lead in all aspects of my life.

All I can say now is: "Be careful what you ask for. You might just get it."

2
The Desolation

It was almost exactly six months later when I sensed that something in my marriage had changed. It was Christmastime, and my wife seemed distant. This was very unusual. We had always enjoyed an intimate relationship and holidays were close family times, especially after the birth of our son Luke. It was December 19th, 2010, and we had attended her parents' Christmas program before going out to finish the last of our Christmas shopping. When we arrived at home, I put Christmas music on as I often did during this time of year, and was feeling the joy of the season. I sought to be affectionate with my wife and, oddly, she avoided me. Again, this was very unusual. After she avoided hugging and kissing opportunities a second time, I confronted her, concerned that something was wrong.

I remember the next moment vividly. It seemed to happen in slow motion. I asked her, "What's wrong with you? I can tell something is wrong." She looked at me with a solemn expression and told me she wasn't sure she still wanted to be married. I looked at her dumbfounded and asked, "You don't love me anymore?" Her reply crushed me. She said she wasn't sure and needed time to figure things out. I let her know immediately how much I loved her and wanted to do whatever it took to make our marriage work, but I could feel her emotionally shutting down.

I kept saying to myself, "This isn't happening. How is this possible?" In total shock, I walked away trying to grasp what just had happened. This was the woman with whom I had planned to spend the rest of my life! Despite the fact we never fought and there didn't seem to be any visible signs of trouble in our marriage, I knew in my spirit that this was serious. I went outside and cried for a solid hour, and then tried to pull myself together. We had a dinner party later that evening with friends and co-workers, but the evening was a total mess. All I wanted to do was to leave the party, sit down and talk with my wife, and to work out whatever had gone wrong.

After the party she really didn't want to talk, so I spent some time in quiet prayer asking God to help me in this desperate moment. After we put our son to bed, I tried to pry open the emotional doors she had closed on me, but there was no reaching her at this point. I stayed up all night begging God to reveal to me what I needed to do to reach her again. When the sun came up, I had not slept a wink and went to work a total wreck. Little did I know, this would be the day I would find out my wife was in love with someone else.

It was shortly after lunch when she revealed the news to me. During an intense argument, she made it clear she had no desire to work on the marriage because her heart simply was not in it anymore. I couldn't believe this was really happening! That night she didn't come home; instead, she took our son and stayed with her parents. I was left at home with no clue as to what transpired over the previous twenty-four hours. None of this made sense. I was so angry with her and with God; I didn't know how I was ever going to trust either one again!

I spent the next several days leading up to Christmas trying to get her to stay in the marriage. I wanted to make it work for the sake of our son and the fourteen years we had spent building a life together. If you have ever experienced someone with a hardened heart, you understand that it was too late. She was emotionally finished and had already decided to leave me, our home and her job. I was not prepared for this outcome because I was certain that God was going to bring her back to me. This would be the moment I would glorify God, forgive her and take her back. Or so I thought.

This, however, was not in her plans. As I watched her drive away from our home the last night she was there, I was totally confused and dumbfounded. Was this what God wanted for me, our son, and our family? How could this be? What was God thinking? I never saw this in the Dave Ramsey book: how to recover when your wife leaves you for a co-worker?

As the realization set in that she was not interested in reconciliation, my emotions quickly changed from denial and hope to anger. Questions began racing through my mind as I started to feel more resentment toward God for not allowing me what I wanted. How was I supposed to trust Him when this was how He rewarded those who followed Him? That night I shook my fist in anger and lashed out in words against the God who, I perceived, just sat back and failed to protect my family! How does a loving God give me a son only to take him away from me fifty percent of the time? You call this unconditional love? Really, God, where is Your love in all of this?

Feeling completely overwhelmed, I fell to the ground and cried out to God, "What do You want from me?" What came over me in the next few minutes I can only describe as euphoria. I felt enveloped by an unseen presence that consumed me. My heart ached with joy as it seemed God Himself had embraced me in His loving arms. I no longer felt overwhelmed with worry or hurt. Instead, I was being comforted by the Love Story God was giving to me. The miracle God placed in me, the Holy Spirit, had captivated me in my moment of weakness. It filled my heart with unexplainable warmth. Without understanding what was happening to me, I got up from my knees, wiped the tears away from my eyes, sat down at my computer and wrote my first prayer thanking God for what was happening to me.

O Heavenly Father,

Thank You for this journey You have set before me. Thank You for every trial and painful tear that has brought me to my knees and shown me how much I need You. In the midst of pain You have brought me close to You, and I am thankful for Your purpose and direction leading my steps.

Lord, I declare Jesus the author of my life and ask with all the power You have granted Him that He uses my hands to bring Glory to Your kingdom in heaven, that He uses my feet and guides my steps, that through Your strength I may carry others and bring Glory to You, that He uses my words to lift the spirits of others and bring healing and comfort to them in times of pain and suffering. Lord Jesus, I humbly submit myself to You to use in this life as You see fit.

In Your sweet and glorious name, amen.

When I sat back and read the prayer to myself, I really didn't understand why on earth I was thanking God for this. But after that night I started to wake up each day and thank God for everything that was happening. Instead of dwelling on my fears and worries, I asked Him to use me and this situation to serve Him and bring glory to His kingdom. Taking the focus off of me and putting it on Him started to change my perspective.

3
The Healing

Over the next month something miraculous started to happen. I began writing daily prayers in an attempt to connect relationally with my Heavenly Father. Prior to this event, anyone close to me will tell you that my writing anything was simply a disaster waiting to happen. My father actually had an invisible graveyard for words I used to create out of my own lack of vocabulary. But as I walked straight toward Jesus, words started to flow out of me, and at times I was taken aback by the emotion coming through what I was writing. A spring of life started to flow in me as I realized that I was finding a true sense of joy walking through this trial with Jesus by my side.

One aspect of my story that I have not yet mentioned has to do with my personal well-being. I had always been an adrenaline junkie. One result of this was a multitude of spinal injuries. Prior to my wife's leaving, I had let my body fall apart and began a life of restricting my normal movements to alleviate pain. I was living in chronic pain and had been researching what options were available to help me. I was told after several MRIs that two back surgeries would be necessary to repair four ruptured and deteriorated discs. The MRIs also revealed a small fracture resulting in a condition called spondylolisthesis that was also contributing to my pain. The worst part is that I was not fighting the good fight: I was not actively trying to keep my body healthy to fight the effects of gravity and aging. My body was deconditioned, which exacerbated my pain. I was mostly inactive and felt somewhat depressed that at the early age of forty-two, I was going to be one of the unfortunate back pain sufferers for the rest of my life.

Now, that being said, I am not sure if it was divine intervention, stress, or a little of both, but most of my back pain went away when my wife left. Without the pain crippling me, all I wanted to do was fight the good fight. At this point, my options were either to let my son watch me crumble in the midst of my trial or stand up and fight. I chose the latter. Every day, I put on my iPod, immersed myself in Christian music, and worked out with weights. After that came 500 daily push-ups and a four to eight mile run. During my workouts, I felt the Holy Spirit touch the deepest and most wounded parts of my soul as the lyrics from the Christian music continually ministered God's Word to me. At times, I was so overcome with emotion that I wore sunglasses just to hide the tears I would shed while running. My workouts now became my daily ritual when the joyful presence of the Holy Spirit would sing life back into my broken soul. The more fit I became the better was my pain tolerance. In addition to the daily exercise, I made a decision to eat a mostly raw, organic diet to reduce inflammation and manage pain.

Six months later, I was competing in "mud runs" and finished my first half marathon. Exercise was now my emotional outlet. It was time I could spend alone with God every day. Most of the prayers in this journal were actually conversations I was having with God while running. Now let me disclose that when I say "conversations with God," I am only saying that I would talk to Him; the answers were simply the way God seemed to be directing my thoughts.

In such a short time, I couldn't believe how my life had changed. I couldn't believe how I had changed. I was happy and joyful, not due to my circumstances, but because, for the first time in my life, I was really trusting where God was leading me. Waking up each day with the knowledge that God was present within me became my peace and comfort. It allowed me to change my perspective as the Holy Spirit was romancing my broken heart. Anger, worry, sorrow, bitterness, and resentment slowly were being washed away as I became aware that it took these tragic circumstances to experience the real, true presence of my Lord and Savior.

I remember hearing a song on K-Love radio by Shawn McDonald called *Rise* which prompted me to write: “There is nothing that comes before me that is greater than the power of Christ that is within me.” I truly believe this to the very core of my being. As my pride crumbled, God was opening my heart to His Love Story (the Holy Spirit), and I could see the essence of my joy was not by mistake, good fortune or the absence of life’s trials. On the contrary, there was something new inside me pointing my heart toward the rhythms of my Savior Jesus, and I was radiating an outward joy toward the world that others in my life were able to see. Most importantly, my son was able to see the reflection of my Savior in me. As I spent a great deal of time praying about this, God continued to soften my heart and strip me of my pride, which in return allowed me to start forgiving my wife for leaving our marriage.

4
The Mirror

Spiritual maturity is a by-product of humility, occurring when we realize life is not about "Me." All around us we find that life can be very humbling, but when trials come our way and turn our lives upside down, how do most of us react? My initial response was to point my finger and blame God and my wife instead of taking the time to look in the mirror. I immediately became the ultimate judge and jury, ready to hand down the harshest sentence on, not just my wife, but also on God. Some people might argue that my humility was brought about by my wife leaving me for another man, but that is not true. What humbled me was the realization that I am by nature a sinner who has spent most of my life hiding from the real me. This became apparent when a close friend watching me struggle with my anger, helped me gain a new perspective.

My friend asked me to buy a solid white shirt and a permanent black marker. On the front of the shirt she wanted me to write in giant bold print, the worst sin I've ever committed against God. Then, continuing on the back of the shirt, she wanted me to write, in giant bold print, the second worst sin I have committed against God. To complete the exercise, she wanted me to write as many sins as I could remember all over the rest of the shirt, and then wear the shirt to work the next day. Immediately, as I started to think about revealing the very essence of who I am to the world, I became terrified. All I could think about was: how was I going to hide the real me from the world? I didn't want every person I know to see all I've done wrong.

As embarrassment and fear radiated from my face, she continued to explain that Jesus took the Cross and spread his arms from East to West taking upon himself all the sins of the world. He did not pick and choose the people he was going to forgive. He spread His arms wide and received all of humanity's sin for all eternity. He was able to do this because He was blameless in the eyes of God. He could open His heart and forgive all of humanity because He was not guarding His own sin. Humanity, on the contrary struggles to extend our arms to forgive others because we are too busy guarding our own sins, hiding our shirts covered in the stains of our past hoping the world cannot see through the solid white facade. In order to forgive, we have to be willing to wear the shirt covered in our sins. It is only then that we can extend our arms wide and show the world who we really are on the inside. Showing the world how much we truly need a Savior reveals our connection to God by our own sins.

My friend looked at me noticing the panic on my face and said, "It's painful when we see who we really are, isn't it? Remember though, when you prepare to go to work tomorrow and put on the shirt covered in your sins, Jesus will tell you, 'Michael, I already wore that shirt for you so I could free you from the burdens of your past. Your sins are not yours to carry anymore. I carried them into the darkness, washed your shirt clean and rose out of the darkness, leaving behind your shame, guilt, unworthiness, anger, resentment and bitterness. God knew that letting you carry your sins would prevent you from fulfilling His purpose for each day. Because of His wisdom and My love for you, you no longer have to carry those burdens. Instead your shirt has permanently been cleaned to prepare your heart to walk in the light of My love and serve My Father each day of your precious life.'"

As I prayed and meditated on this truth for several days, God continued to shed His wisdom on my ailing soul. I began to understand more clearly that my connection to God is not built on my good works, but on my weaknesses and sin. The more I was able to focus on my own sin and need for God, as well as how close it brought me to him, the less I was able to point my finger at my wife and judge her for the choices she had made.

As so eloquently said in the movie, *Shrek*, "Ogres have layers." So also, do people, and it would behoove all of us to spend time peeling back the layers of life to be able to see the picture God is painting for us. About a week after my friend challenged me to wear the white shirt covered in my sins; I spent an afternoon with my brother-in-law. He is a pastor, and I was in need of spiritual and emotional guidance. In truth, what I really wanted was someone to tell me I was right and the anger I was feeling inside was okay. I wanted someone to help me justify my feelings of disappointment, loss, anger, and bitterness that attacked me every day.

Following our customary "hellos" and a brief acknowledgment as to what happened between my wife and me; I was a little surprised that he didn't seem to take my side. Instead, he encouraged me to take this opportunity to look at myself in the mirror. He asked me to reflect on the impact the presence of the Holy Spirit had made on my life since this journey began. I explained to him that it had brought me closer to God than I had ever been in my life and opened my heart to a real relationship with Jesus. I continued to explain that this entire experience, although difficult, had begun a transformation in me that was life changing. At this point, I was feeling pretty good about how I had taken this disaster in stride. Then, out of nowhere, he hit me with truth that was like swallowing dry sand.

"If that is so Michael, then you must love them both [my wife and the man she left me for] as God loves them." Tears immediately started to flow as a deep ache grew in the pit of my stomach. I knew he was right, but getting there was so difficult.

It was in this moment that I realized how I was still trying to control my emotions. Despite the progress I felt I had made, along with the spiritual closeness I was feeling toward God, I was still trying to control my healing. I had not completely let down my walls allowing God to transform me fully through this trial. Now, it was time to peel back the layers and take a deeper look at myself and what had happened to me during the last three months. It was time to tear down the walls I have built and walk straight toward God. There needed to be no boundaries. I simply needed to get over myself and start putting my trust in God and the miracle of my Savior who was touching the deepest parts of my broken heart.

Peeling back the layers of life, however, can feel like sharp knives cutting through the empty facades, revealing truths that don't seem to fit into the little boxes that make up our spiritual philosophies. In other words, it is much easier for us to make Jesus fit into the mold we create that is most convenient for the lives we want to live, instead of allowing His love to transform us into living the life God wants us to live.

Despite the progress I was making spiritually, I had many setbacks. Each time anger rose up in me, I would feel like I had failed God. One morning, I was experiencing an overwhelming sense of unworthiness, as God had been revealing all that Jesus had suffered for me. Fighting anger toward what had happened to me and the feelings of failure to overcome it, I cried out to God…

Dear Jesus,

Why did You give your life for me? Why do I, in all my brokenness, matter to You? Why do You care about me and my soul? Have You not seen what I have done? I am so unworthy of Your love and ashamed of every sin that You took to the Cross for me. Why did You do this for me, Jesus? I just can't see God's wisdom in letting You die for my sins. Who am I, and why does the Maker of the Universe who has seen all I have done not just cast me out into the darkness. Please help me understand, Jesus; why do You love me? WHY?

This is what the Holy Spirit led me to write in response:

Oh my son, there is so much left for you to learn about God's love and His divine wisdom. The miracle I represent is not just the sacrifice I suffered for you to free you from your burdens. It is also the power of your submission to my spirit that lives within you.

When I went to sit at the right hand of my Father in Heaven, I left behind a power that exceeds time and is everlasting. The Cross was a burden I had to bear for you my child, so I could release you of your burdens and free you of your chains. I cannot make you whole if you are lost in shame, guilt, fear, and a sense of unworthiness. These thoughts give power to Satan as he tries to suppress the miracle of Me in you. You must know that I have already claimed this victory over him to remove his power from you so you can feel My presence resting in your heart and free yourself of any strong hold he has over your life.

Doubts are times in your life when you are not focused on Me, on the miracle inside that frees you of all your self-doubt, suppressing Satan and allowing My Spirit to guide your steps toward a full life. Through Me you have no limits and can accomplish all that my Father lays at your feet. If you doubt My love for you, the power of My spirit that dwells in your heart and the purpose of the Cross, you give power to the darkness that wants to separate Me from you. You are My child whom I have chosen for a specific purpose—to serve My Father's Kingdom. I have laid down My life so you can be free of the strong hold of darkness that would rule the world. You must spend time with Me everyday to strengthen our bond and push the darkness out to allow the light of My spirit to lead the way. As our time together grows, people in your life will no longer see your reflection of self doubt, shame, guilt, fear and unworthiness. Instead they will begin to see My reflection radiate outwardly. The purpose and miracle of the Cross is revealed as you are transformed by My love. You will begin to see that the sacrifice I made for you was so I could live through you and bring glory to My Father in Heaven.

The answer to the question that troubles you is simple: the sacrifice I made for you was the price I had to pay for My spirit to live actively in you. This miracle is timeless and directs all who call on My name, which gives power to My Father in Heaven to work His divine plan through all eternity. Rest in me and find peace, knowing that I love you my child and trust My Spirit that lives in you guiding your steps and working My Father's miracles through your wondrous hands.

These words revealed the picture of God I believe He wanted me to see, but the healing came when I realized the words I wrote weren't meant for just me, but for everyone. God wanted me to radiate His grace and mercy toward those who have hurt me to show how His love had transformed me. Up to this point, I had taken baby steps, but now it was time to stop playing god and judging the world for the wrongs committed against me. It was time to begin to see the world through the eyes of my Savior.

Despite knowing this intellectually, why was it so difficult to forgive my wife and just move forward? When I peeled back the spiritual layers, I started to see my pride taking center stage, blocking my ability to forgive. I was trapped in a vicious circle, emotionally acting as if God had forgiven me for my sins, but not those who had sinned against me. This never ending cycle of playing god, but failing to forgive the sinner, was putting my own faith in Christ on trial. When I perceived that sins were being committed against me, I immediately switched into god-mode. Instead of showing mercy; I began to condemn the sinner. One night, trapped in this cycle of failure to forgive as I had been forgiven, I fell to my knees, stretched my arms to heaven, and called for God to reach down to me and lift me out of this pit of despair. As a follower of Christ, I knew that I was called to forgive, but why did it feel like this time was different? I felt that I had been betrayed and left heartbroken. Doesn't that count for some type of punishment? As those thoughts seemed to dominate my mind, I felt these words touch my heart:

> *Michael, you cannot wash anyone clean of their sins; only I can and have already done so through the sacrifice of My Son. He was My love offering to the world to take away the burdens carried by men for all sin. He is the essence of true love and, because of His love for you and obedience to Me, the world has been given the perfect picture of what My heart desires for all. You need to humble yourself to the gift I have given you—to forgive and show mercy toward others who have hurt you to reciprocate My love offering for your own sins.*

> **Mark 11:25** And when you stand praying, if you hold anything against anyone, forgive him, so that your Father in heaven may forgive you your sins.

This amazing Love Story that captivated my broken heart during the darkest time in my life had taken every burden on my heart to the grave and rose victorious over it; He had also taken every sin that I felt had been committed against me. This was the challenging part of the healing process: letting go of my pride and realizing I have to forgive those who have sinned against me. God did not place the burden of atonement for the sins of others upon my shoulders. If the burden of atonement is not placed on my shoulders to wash clean anyone else's sin, then is sin actually committed against me, or against God? My prideful human nature wants to point out the wrongs done to me, put someone on trial, and then have them receive the punishment I believe they deserve. Forgiveness isn't my first instinct when I am more concerned about receiving my justice than I am in showing mercy. This was eye opening to me because it showed me clearly how far my heart was from God. I wanted to feel close to God and align my heart with His. But when it was my time to let my Savior radiate out from me, my pride wanted to rule the day, hold back mercy and wave the heavy hand of justice.

Again struggling mightily, I asked God to help me let go, and this is what I was led to write:

> *Michael, I am in you, through the amazing Gift that I placed within you. The peace you are seeking is found when you humble yourself to this Gift and are able to show mercy and forgiveness as I have done so for you. My wisdom is found when you follow My will and free your heart of the burdens of life. You will also show the world the reflection of My Son, and they will see that He is alive and in you. You must now submit to His spirit and let Him love through you. Let His mercy out and show the world the Light of My Son through your actions. As you submit to My Spirit and show grace and mercy, you will be healing the wounds of your own heart and you will bring glory to Me. Then the love I have for you will be found and your desire to show your son the heart of Jesus will be revealed.*

Left crying on floor, I could feel my heart begin to change as I started to understand more clearly what God wanted from me. The bitterness that had been dominating my thoughts started to fade away and I could feel a sense of peace overcome me. The wisdom of my loving Savior was being revealed to me through my own need to show mercy.

As I lay there on the floor, I remembered the day my son was born and I had prayed that my son would be able to see Jesus in me. Finally it hit me—I realized this was the moment that by showing mercy I could reveal to my son that Jesus was alive and living through me. Tears let loose as I completely let go and, for the second time in a year, I was enveloped by euphoria as His love washed over me. I sat there on the floor, unable to move, feeling the power and freedom of completely surrendering my burdens to God. All of the pieces to the puzzle started to come together as God opened my eyes to the picture He was painting.

As difficult as it was to watch my son suffer the wounds of divorce, I had to lose my wife in order to find myself broken enough to be stripped of my pride. God then revealed Himself to me through the Holy Spirit, and I have fallen in love with Jesus.

5
A New Me

One of the most troubling questions to those who believe in an all-loving God is: Why does God allow us to suffer? Sometimes the answer to that question requires more than a one-second synopsis that "all things happen for a reason" or "God has a plan for us." Those simple answers aren't good enough to explain the trials that come our way, especially when we are suffering through tremendous emotional and sometimes physical pain.

When I began this trial, life left me lost and broken. I felt stripped of my identity and unaware of the miracle God had residing in me. Not knowing how I was going to get through each day, God revealed Himself to me. I then, turned to Him and prayed that He would help me grow through it. When I experienced His love touch me, my heart changed. I could see it took a tragedy of this magnitude to strip me of my pride and find myself broken enough to let God transform me. Now I do not claim to know what God's wisdom is for anyone apart from me, but I do believe He desires for us to turn our hearts toward His Love Story and let Him heal us. As I started to put my life back together I wrote this next paragraph to explain to myself why this had happened to me:

If you take your hands and interlock your fingers, one hand represents you and the other is your pride. When life's trials rip us apart, the hand which is our pride falls to the ground. God's divine plan is to remake us through Christ. Too many of us fail to look for God's Love Story inside ourselves to help us to heal. Instead, our prideful nature reaches down and picks up the broken pieces and adds the old prideful pieces back to who we are. We, at that moment, fail to allow the purpose of the Cross to transform us. I feel that, when life breaks us, it is God's plan to make us in His image by turning us away from our pride, our brokenness. As we turn from pride and find humility, we allow God the opportunity to add the pieces of Christ to who we are. We then begin our spiritual transformation from brokenness to completeness through His love, grace and humility. This miracle of transformation resides in all of us when we are willing to surrender ourselves to the Holy Spirit and let His joy transform the world around us. Our trials then become part of His plan as we bring our Savior down from the Cross and He comes alive in us. The victory is our witness as God heals our wounds and transforms His world through us.

This entire journey led me to two passages of scripture. The first I have already mentioned:

> **Mark 11:25** And when you stand praying, if you hold anything against anyone, forgive him, so that your Father in heaven may forgive you your sins.

The second verse represented my spiritual transformation. It revealed to me that reconciliation is not always a process of restoring what once was, but more the process of becoming one with God through submission of self-pride. To be reconciled with God through my own admission of sin acknowledges my limitations as a human and a need for a Savior. It allows me to be transformed, not through my own strength, but through the acknowledgment of my weaknesses. Through this process I then become a new creation in Christ. Therefore, it is no longer possible to restore what once was because I am no longer who I was before. Reconciliation is not the process of restoring what you had, but creating something completely new in likeness of our God. To be reconciled in our relationships is the process of allowing ourselves to submit first to the Spirit of God that lives in each of us. In Him lie the secrets to forgiveness. Through our own submission to Him, our hearts will gain the wisdom to be reconciled to each other. Love is found hiding behind our pride, showing us how to be loved and how to love. It is my prayer that God will show all who read this the power of scripture.

> **2 Corinthians 5:17-18** Therefore, if anyone is in Christ, the new creation has come: The old has gone, the new is here! All this is from God, who reconciled us to himself through Christ and gave us the ministry of reconciliation[.]

6

No One Said the Journey Would be Easy, Just Worth it

When my wife left the marriage, I felt like a total failure. I watched fourteen years of life literally walk right out the door. I thought that my self-esteem and self-worth were damaged beyond repair and I was struggling to find my identity. I was so defeated I actually told my wife after she left me I didn't think any other woman would be interested in a forty-three-year-old, broken-down man.

Thankfully, as you have followed me along this journey, you know that mindset didn't last long because God reached down and rescued me. He revealed His Love Story in the Holy Spirit and pointed my heart in the direction I needed to look to find my identity. There is great wisdom in understanding that our identity is not found in the things of this world because, when they are taken away either by death, divorce, financial struggle, or job loss, what is left of us? Our identity is not found in our spouse, children, job, or even success; it is found in our Savior, Jesus. Nothing can separate us from His love.

> **Romans 8:35-39** Who shall separate us from the love of Christ? Shall trouble or hardship or persecution or famine or nakedness or danger or sword? As it is written: "For your sake we face death all day long; we are considered as sheep to be slaughtered." No, in all these things we are more than

> conquerors through him who loved us. For I am convinced that neither death nor life, neither angels nor demons, neither the present nor the future, nor any powers, neither height nor depth, nor anything else in all creation, will be able to separate us from the love of God that is in Christ Jesus our Lord.

He is my rock, my foundation, and the direction my heart seeks for happiness. He carries me into valleys and rejoices with me on the hilltops. I am truly thankful for every tear I shed in writing this journal, for the Love Story I found between me and my Maker and the wisdom God revealed to me to let go of myself and look to the miracle inside me for my identity.

Growing closer to God is a process of giving up control. I have learned that I am a fragile creature fighting a constant battle for control with a patient and loving God. This journey helped me realize that I am in control of only one thing and that is how I choose to respond to what happens to me every day. I need not devote any energy in trying to control anyone else's emotions or reactions. My energy must be committed to surrendering to the Holy Spirit for guidance in order to find peace in the midst of life's storms. When I learned to commit my energy toward that goal, I found that God not only brought me peace, but He also used me to minister to other people in my life, showing them the glory of healing through His grace in me.

God's grace opened my eyes to the devastating power of failing to forgive. Through friends, family, and the Divorce Care program, I have heard heartbreaking stories of wounded parents putting pride and ego before the fragile emotional nature of their children. This affected me deeply and helped point my heart toward my Savior for guidance during some of the more difficult moments during the separation and divorce. I am thankful that I asked God every day to protect my heart from the emotional disease of failure to forgive so I would not pass those wounds onto my son nor carry them into my future. This daily prayer served me well as my son is now prospering in a challenging bilingual elementary school program and I have been able to rebuild a working relationship with my former wife so that we are able to co-parent our son well together.

Grace and forgiveness are only a part of God's wisdom; when I learned to let go of each day and live according to how the Spirit was leading me, I was showing God that I trusted Him. When I learned the power found in trusting God, it was truly transformational for me. The burdens each day no longer stuck to me and everything that came my way just seemed smaller and less significant. I could feel His Spirit strengthening me since I was no longer consumed with worry. Wondering how I was going to make it to the next day was replaced with looking forward to the possibilities of what God was going to show me and how He was going to use me to help others. All I wanted to do was serve Him and it truly changed my perspective on how I approached each new day.

Despite the strength I felt spiritually, I still had doubts that I would be able to allow myself to love again with an open and truly vulnerable heart. Reflecting on my journey, I have to laugh because God never seems to follow my plans. I remember a quote by Woody Allen that made me laugh out loud: "If you want to make God laugh, tell him your plans."

If I have learned anything from this journey it has been that you never know what tomorrow will bring. Before I knew what hit me, a new woman entered my life, captured my heart, and tore down all my walls of doubt. Because I believed in the healing power of the Cross, I was able to let myself be vulnerable again. Although I knew the risks associated with what that meant, God showed me that love was worth it.

So I trusted God and allowed myself to love someone again. As we began conversations about marriage, life showed us how cruel it can be. This wonderful new woman in my life was diagnosed with an extremely rare and potentially fatal cancer. Despite the immediate shock, my spirit wasn't overwhelmed. This was emotionally more devastating than the loss of my marriage, but now I was in a different place spiritually. Simply put, I was not trying to control the outcome of her cancer. I gave it to God and trusted that whatever happened would draw us closer to each other and to Him. Instead of anxiety, stress, and the multitude of questions that hit me when my former wife left our marriage, this time God covered me with His peace. Even with the looming surgery to remove the cancer and the results of the final pathology, I knew everything was going to be okay.

I am thankful to be able to write that the surgery to remove the cancer was successful, and we were married exactly eight weeks later. The journey we have taken together since that time has strengthened our love for each other and has brought us closer together. I truly believe God prepared us for each other to share in the challenges and joys of life together. Although it feels like we have been on a roller coaster, riding the highs and lows life has thrown at us, through it all I have been able to carry forward the lessons God taught me when my former wife left and thank Him through this entire process.

Life is full of ups and downs, but the peace He gives me no matter what life throws at me simply comes from the trust I put in Him every day. For me, today only has one purpose and that is simply to draw me nearer to God. This has been one of the greatest gifts I have learned along this journey—trust. There is peace that comes from understanding that I am not here for life to serve me, but rather, I am here to serve God. He understands how hard life is and has given me an amazing gift to lean on during the hard times that are sure to come my way. It is up to me to lay aside my pride and let God live through me. When I am able to let go, I am overcome with peace.

I wanted to share this wisdom with my son, so I wrote this prayer for him—"The Morning Prayer".

> *O Heavenly Father,*
>
> *I give my heart to You today and will walk by faith that what is before me is your divine plan to bring me closer to You. Help me to always see and feel the joyful light of Christ that You've placed in me to be my first love and great companion. Thank You for this day. May it be all Yours to teach me Your Grace, Mercy, and Love!*
>
> *In Christ's name, I pray! Amen!*

This prayer is a summation of what God has taught me so far and reflects the spiritual wisdom I want to share with my son as his earthly father. In short, the prayer says that when I wake up I will give my heart to God and trust that each day has only one purpose, whether it is good day or bad day, and that is to draw me nearer to God. God knew life would be full of challenges, so He gave me the gift of Christ in the Holy Spirit as my joyful companion to strengthen me through the darkness and to rejoice with me on the hilltops. This day is no longer mine, but it is His to teach me all that is good within me to share with those He has placed in my life. May I serve Him in all that I do and learn what it means to love others like He loves me.

7
The Four Keys to Healing

Writing this journal was an ongoing conversation I was having with God. It was a spiritual journey that led me toward healing. I believe a short explanation of how God directed my thoughts as I wrote this journal will give you a better understanding as you read through the following prayers.

I believe that during life's trials, it is easy to allow our thoughts to be led away from the healing power of God's love. There is in all of us a certain amount of darkness, but it is the light in us that gives way to life. I have come to believe that the darkness that lives in us comes from Satan, who desires that we not heal from the pain that life presents us, that we not turn to the light God put in us. Satan desires that we isolate ourselves from God and live in anger, resentment, bitterness, and failure to forgive. If we allow Satan to have this victory, then the purpose and love of the Cross is lost to us. In order to avoid this, we must turn to God's Word that teaches us how to cope with difficult times.

First, Jesus teaches us this from His own trial in the desert, that God did not desire we endure the darkness of life alone. Even as God on earth, Jesus did not rely upon Himself and His own powers; instead He looked to His Father and submitted to His will to overcome His time in the desert. So Jesus teaches us clearly that we cannot overcome the darkness of life on our own. We must turn to God, and rely on His strength to get us through difficult times.

Second, the faith of the Israelites was put to the test during their forty years in the desert. Often it is the testing we endure that determines the strength of our faith and our true character. A student once asked his teacher, "What is the purpose of taking a test anyway—to determine how much we know?" The teacher replied, "No, it is to determine how much you still need to learn." When we are tested in the trials of life, our trials then become our opportunity to strengthen our faith and grow closer to God.

Third, God in His divine wisdom knows that part of our spiritual journey is learning to persevere with a joyful heart. We all know someone who, through very difficult circumstances, handled themselves with grace, humility and joy. They inspire families, towns, cities, and even nations with the way they handle their circumstances and persevere. When through our faith we demonstrate trust in God and persevere with a joyful heart, we ultimately grow closer to Him.

Also, when we experience the presence and peace of the Holy Spirit during our trials we become aware that our joy comes from this Love Story God has placed in us. Learning to be joyful is not related to what the world offers me. It is the realization that God put a little piece of Himself in me. When I wake up and realize the power of the Holy Spirit lives in me, I will always be joyful. This is one of the greatest spiritual gifts God has given all of us.
Finally, the greatest part of spiritual maturity is thankfulness. This lesson in God's great plan was actually revealed to me before I began this journey as I watched a wonderful, godly woman give her life to God as a living example of the Gospel when she was diagnosed with terminal cancer. Her life verse was:

> **1 Thessalonians 5:16-18** Rejoice always, pray continually, give thanks in all circumstances; for this is God's will for you in Christ Jesus.

She truly trusted that God blessed her with cancer to provide an opportunity for her to share the love of Christ with everyone she met. She knew that we would all take notice and listen to someone in her circumstances. What was so amazing about her was the impact she had the moment you met her. She captivated you with the way she carried the Gospel. What was always most important to her was: How are you doing? How is God working in your life? How is He blessing you? Not a word was ever spoken about her cancer, how she was feeling, or how her treatment was going. She simply wouldn't allow it. I knew her for only a short time, but she changed my life forever. Her faith showed me that God will use all circumstances. He desires that we seek His wisdom and learn to trust His judgment that what is set before us is part of a divine plan to draw us closer to Him.

What I have come to understand is that I affect those around me and they are watching how I handle life. Ultimately, if I awake each day knowing God in His divine plan put the light of His glorious Son in me, I will always be thankful. If the peace and grace of Christ shine through me, I will transform other lives around me as they see the light of Christ in me, handling each day with grace, humility, joy and thankfulness. When you sit and meditate on this, you will be able to see God's wisdom in Christ and the purpose of allowing yourself to be transformed by Him through your trials. The lessons found in each day reveal not obstacles, but opportunities to show this dark world that the joyful light of Christ will prevail over the trials of life.

8
Moving Forward

I would like to provide some additional guidance before you begin reading through the forty prayers. These prayers were not designed to be read all at once, but more so, one per day over a forty day period. The prayers do follow a basic theme; leaning on God, revealing your weaknesses, finding your joy, and trusting God, but they can be read in any order. You have the flexibility to read the prayers that are related to the area in your life with which you are struggling now. Each prayer is named, giving you the purpose and meaning of the prayer. As you will see, the prayers are a reflection of the constant battle that raged inside me between my pride and the healing power of the Holy Spirit. The prayers spoke to me with a voice of reason and love, and, as I wrote them, they helped to point my heart in the direction of God's healing and steered me away from my prideful ego. Healing is a roller coaster ride of emotions and everyone heals at a different pace. You don't just wake up one day and find you're healed; instead, you will have good days and bad days, days of anger and sadness, and days of joy. Regardless of where your journey begins, healing is a process and will take time as you learn to trust God and seek guidance from the Holy Spirit.

I think it is very important for you to understand as you read through the prayers, that writing them may not have changed my circumstances, but it did change my perspective. It helped me see that life really is less what you make it, and more how you choose to take it.

Who am I, and what has become of my life? Am I the product of the Spirit God put in me, or am I the product of a broken world? Because we are all truly the aftermath of our life's experiences, we must at some point choose to allow God's Love Story to heal us or permit the darkness of this broken world to pull us away from His healing love. What came to me as I began this journey was that out of the aftermath of my Savior's death came the greatest gift to mankind. Through His suffering, His pain, the physical wounds He endured for us, and ultimately His death, God in this beautiful love story gave me life. Out of the aftermath of Jesus' suffering and death, God placed a miracle in me. Therefore, if I turn to this miracle for healing, I can, in return, share this light with others!

PART TWO

The Prayers

9

Leaning on God

DAY 1 CONNECTING TO THE FATHER'S LOVE

O Heavenly Father,

Why do You love me? Why do You care about my heart, my burdens, and my wounds?

I am so lost in myself that I cannot hear Your voice speak to me. I have spent too much time sitting on my own throne and not enough time listening to You guide my steps. My priorities are not in order, and I am watching my life slip away, caught up in a world that cannot fill a single gap of emptiness that lingers in my heart. Life has taught me hard lessons about the broken world that desires only to tear me away from You.

As I sit here in misery, heartbroken, lost in myself, and alone, You have opened my heart to Your presence in me, and I can see a distant light. Your voice in my heart tells me to get off my throne, humble myself, and cry out to You. On my floor I give my soul to You, a mercy cry from my broken spirit, left damaged by the battles of this empty world. Suddenly, a warmth covers me as Your Spirit, for the first time in my true humbleness, lets me know you are here, not because You have ever been absent, but because my pride kept me from experiencing You. That little light and the presence of Your spirit gives me hope to make it to the next day. Although I am weak, I begin each day with my battle cry to You, and You are strengthening my spirit. It is not through pride, but through humbleness. Your strength is amazing to me and I know now I cannot make this journey on my own. You are the only real true source that is life giving. Thank You for allowing me to humble myself long enough to experience the Maker of the universe touching my heart. Help me, Oh Lord, to find out all that I am in Christ so I can realize why You created me and I can bring glory to You.

In Christ's name I pray, amen.

> **Romans 5:2-5** [T]hrough whom we have gained access by faith into this grace in which we now stand. And we boast in the hope of the glory of God. Not only so, but we also glory in our sufferings, because we know that suffering produces perseverance; perseverance, character; and character, hope. And hope does not put us to shame, because God's love has been poured out into our hearts through the Holy Spirit, who has been given to us.

When your heart is broken, each day becomes more about surviving than living. This was where I found myself as I first struggled to connect to my Heavenly Father's love. It was all about surviving; actually living out my days seemed impossible. Emotionally I wasn't capable of waking up with a passion to look forward to what the day would bring. Every heartbeat felt like I had a 300-pound weight sitting on my chest and it took all my strength just to breathe. My mind kept running in circles. Fear and anger had overcome my spirit as my pride took center stage. At this point, I wasn't drawing nearer to God, I was pushing Him away.

No matter what I tried, I couldn't fix it. I wanted my wife back, but in all my cleverness I wasn't able to say the right words, manipulate reality, and get her to come back home. Frustration and desperation are a tired place to be at the end of each day, especially when you are trying to control everything. You end up leaving nothing to give to the areas of your life that need your attention the most. For me, that was my son. He needed me to be strong and stay in the game, but this was when my spirit was weakest.

I am so thankful that when my "wake up moment" finally came, I was ready to put down my pride and listen to the Spirit of God. During this dark moment in my life, I could feel His Spirit moving my heart toward Him. Every ounce of fear that had been consuming my thoughts started to fade away. My mind finally stopped racing in circles and I could feel the Holy Spirit bring me back to life. It is important to note here, that despite the intensity of God's love I could feel leading me, I struggled daily, but now I wasn't doing it alone.

DAY 2 LEARNING TO TRUST AGAIN

O Heavenly Father,

Trust is a daily walk, a conflict, between the world telling me what I am supposed to feel and You designing a future that brings glory to Yourself in all circumstances. It is difficult to wait for the story You have scripted for me. Please be patient while my trust in You is growing. I have only begun to stick my toes in the water because I want to believe that You are in control and ready to carry me. Life is teaching me that there is a plan I cannot fully understand. I must learn to live out the journey giving each day to You. I know we all die, but we all don't live. True living is dying to myself each day and allowing the gift of Your Spirit to lead my steps through the hardships and joys of life. As the pages of my life's journey are turning, each new day is an opportunity to trust Your plan for my life. It is simply establishing a dependence on You and trusting that each day, no matter what comes my way, is an opportunity to learn more about Your love and grow closer to You. I ask You, Lord, with all the power You have given Jesus, to strengthen my trust in You and allow Him to live through me so I may be one of those who truly live.

In Christ's name I pray, amen.

1 Peter 5:7 Cast all your anxiety on Him because He cares for you.

Psalms 13:5 But I trust in your unfailing love; my heart rejoices in your salvation.

One of the hardest parts of walking through trials is learning to trust God. At first, I felt God betrayed me, but, as things in my life played out, I started to understand more clearly the path I was on. Early on, one of the saddest revelations I had was realizing I had not made it a priority to teach my son about Jesus. Once I experienced His love, I had a fire burning inside me to share my love for Christ with my son.

Each day was a new opportunity to talk with him about what I was experiencing inside. "Make Christ known to him" was my mantra. This previously had been the passion of my wife to teach our son about Christ, but now it was my heart's desire to assume that role in his life.

About a week after she left, I was driving from work listening to K-LOVE radio when a song by Sanctus Real called, *Lead Me,* left me sitting in my car crying for almost an hour. Here are the lyrics from the first verse of the song:

> *I look around and see my wonderful life*
> *Almost perfect from the outside*
> *In picture frames I see my beautiful wife*
> *Always smiling*
> *But on the inside, I can hear her saying...*
>
> *Lead me with strong hands*
> *Stand up when I can't*
> *Don't leave me hungry for love*
> *Chasing dreams, what about us?*
> *Show me you're willing to fight*
> *That I'm still the love of your life*
> *I know we call this our home*
> *But I still feel alone*

It was if these words had been written just for me to hear. I didn't lead my wife or my son spiritually and the result was the loss of my family. I let the enemy in and he stole them right out from under me. It was a hard pill to swallow emotionally. I decided that night I was never going to sit back and passively let the enemy take from me anymore. For the rest of my life I was going to assume the role of teaching my son about Jesus and that's exactly what I've done.

Several months later, I was taking my son to stay at my mother's house for an afternoon before heading off for a long run. Out of nowhere, my son asked me, "Daddy, do you know how I show I love you?" I said, "Tell me buddy." "I like to do things for you, Daddy." I said to him, "That's sweet buddy, do you know how I show you I love you?" Now I was going to give him a long list of all the things I do for him, but he quickly replied, "Yes, Daddy, you teach me about Jesus." I immediately started to cry. I realized in that moment everything I had suffered over the previous five months was worth it to hear those words come from his mouth. I looked up to heaven as I pulled into my mom's driveway, closed my eyes, and said, "Lord, I trust You."

DAY 3 LETTING GO OF PRIDE

O Heavenly Father,

Forgive me, for I have tried to make Christ fit the mold that seems to appeal to my nature. Yet You have commanded that I learn to die every day so Christ can live through me. Lord, I have watched men and women all around me, including myself, trying to add Jesus to who we are rather than emptying ourselves to become who Christ wants us to be. I realize now that I cannot serve You when I am serving myself. I am beginning to learn that I will, by my own nature, serve myself first unless I lay at Your feet my selfish ways. Why am I so rebellious and prideful? How I long to live in a closer relationship with You, but seem so unwilling to come to Your table and set aside my agenda that I might receive Your perfect will. I ask with all the power You have given Jesus to awaken the Holy Spirit in me. Remind me, Lord, that I must spend time with You every day, learning that the selfless death of my will for Yours opens my heart to be in the fullness of Your divine love and wisdom. Please allow the light of Christ to heal my wounds and shine His love on all those who have wronged me so I may receive Your full forgiveness of my own sin. Let the light of Christ shine bright within me, O Lord.

In Christ's name I pray, amen.

Leviticus 26:19 I will break down your stubborn pride and make the sky above you like iron and the ground beneath you like bronze.

Proverbs 11:2 When pride comes, then comes disgrace, but with humility comes wisdom.

DAY 4 LEAD ME IN THE SPIRIT

O Heavenly Father,

While I am asleep and my mind is quiet, remind me how much I need to trust You. Bind me to the Holy Spirit, my wondrous gift and constant companion. Lead my thoughts with the Spirit's continual guidance, nudging my heart in the path of Your will. Reveal to me Your never ending and all consuming knowledge that this trial is my opportunity to grow closer to You. You know the beginning and the end and I must place my trust in You that this day is Yours. No matter where I am on my journey, remind me that You have already walked the steps and are preparing for me a new day filled with abundant life that flows from trusting our precious Savior. I pray, Lord, as my trust in You continues to grow, that others in my life will come to know You simply by the reflection of You they see in me. Lord, I humbly submit myself and my body to You, trusting that You will use this day and my circumstances to bring glory to Your Kingdom.

In Christ's sweet and holy name I pray, amen.

Isaiah 40:31 [B]ut those who hope in the Lord will renew their strength. They will soar on wings like eagles; they will run and not grow weary, they will walk and not be faint.

Romans 8:31-32 What, then, shall we say in response to these things? If God is for us, who can be against us? He who did not spare His own Son, but gave Him up for us all, how will He not also, along with Him, graciously give us all things?

DAY 5 STEPPING OUT OF THE BOAT

O Heavenly Father,

You have called me to step out into the storm and trust that You will not only guide my steps, but also lead me to a place of extraordinary peace. You have wrapped Your love around me and I am overwhelmed by how my faith is growing every day. I know I am planted right here, right now, for You and Your glory alone. You are continuing to call me to step out of my boat of comfort and trust all that is laid before me is directed to serve You for Your divine purpose. Asking me to Trust You will bring glory to You out of difficult circumstances. As my eyes are open to Your presence in me, I am learning that the pains I have suffered during this difficult trial are part of Your plan to heal me through our glorious Savior, Jesus. The wisdom I have found in Your Son has shown me that life's pains are opportunities to feel Christ's constant presence healing the wounds of my heart, planting the seeds of love and forgiveness, leading me toward a future You have planned for me that I cannot imagine. This knowledge has given me peace that was lacking before my painful trial began. Thank You, Lord, for every step I have taken that has opened my heart to You, and for directing me along this journey You planned for me long ago. I know that if all I am is in You, I will always be okay!

In Christ's glorious name I pray, amen.

MATTHEW 19:26 Jesus looked at them and said, "With man this is impossible, but with God all things are possible."

It is important to remember that healing is not an instantaneous process. It comes gradually as you are ready to let go. From a spiritual point of view, letting go is really all about trusting God. However, when emotional pain hits, that is easier said than done. It is so hard to just give it all to God, but that is what God demands we do.

Matthew 14:25-32 Shortly before dawn Jesus went out to them, walking on the lake. When the disciples saw him walking on the lake, they were terrified. "It's a ghost," they said, and cried out in fear. But Jesus immediately said to them: "Take courage! It is I. Don't be afraid." "Lord, if it's you," Peter replied, "tell me to come to you on the water." "Come," he said. Then Peter got down out of the boat, walked on the water and came toward Jesus. But when he saw the wind, he was afraid and, beginning to sink, cried out, "Lord, save me!" Immediately Jesus reached out his hand and caught him. "You of little faith," he said, "why did you doubt?" And when they climbed into the boat, the wind died down. Then those who were in the boat worshiped him, saying, "Truly you are the Son of God."

What stands out to me in this story is not that Jesus walked on water, but rather that Peter lost his faith as he began his own journey toward Jesus. No matter how strong your faith may be, doubt will always creep in. The enemy wants to separate you from the Holy Spirit. He wants you to stumble, doubt, and hurt those you love the most.

I had one of those moments when I needed to walk toward Jesus and not let my pride get the best of me. It was on a Monday night when I would normally pick up my son at his mother's apartment. He was having a hard time understanding our separation and didn't want to leave her apartment. These are the hard times, watching my son cry because he wanted to stay with her and not come home with me. That really hurt me emotionally, but I had to remember that this situation is not his fault. So that night on our ride home he told me he didn't want to stay with me, but wanted to go back and stay with his mother. Then, he asked if it was okay for him to feel that way. As much as it hurt to hear those words, I told him it was okay to feel that way, but I was not going to change the schedule. I did, however, let him know he always has the right to express his feelings to me.

For children going through divorce, it is difficult for them emotionally because they have no control over the circumstances. Their entire lives are being ripped apart and the worlds they have always known are now turned upside down. It is crucial at this point in the process that the two people they love deeply must let go of their pride and simply confirm their children's feelings. This is so challenging for parents, especially if they have been hurt, because our pride urges us to be right more so than do right. Our pride urges us to make the other parent the reason for all the problems. Emotionally, it may seem like the right thing to do, but how does a child process complex emotions? The child loves both parents; therefore, identifying one of them to be the problem only adds additional stress to an already fragile child. What worked for me was to let my son know that what he was feeling was okay. Just giving him confirmation about how he felt seemed to defuse the emotional struggle he had on the inside.

These emotional struggles are the hardest times. I would encourage all parents going through separation and divorce to keep your eyes on Jesus. Remember to let Him speak through you. Take a moment when your feelings are hurt, reach out to God for guidance, and don't allow yourself to react out of hurt to what is happening. Let the Spirit guide you and show your children exactly the right way to handle conflict.

DAY 6 BE COURAGEOUS

O Heavenly Father,

I am opening my heart to your awesome power and beginning to see that it is Your light within me that flows forth like a spiritual river into a dark world that thirsts to taste the love of Christ. Lord, I am weak in my flesh and fearful that I will fall short of the tasks You place at my feet. Your word tells me:

Deuteronomy 31:6 Be strong and courageous. Do not be afraid or terrified because of them, for the Lord Your God goes with you; He will never leave you or forsake you.

Lord, I humbly ask, with all the power you have granted Jesus, that You drop the walls of pride in me and allow Him to take control of my life, lifting away the fears that keep me from serving you. I am thankful for your opening my eyes to the glorious gift of Christ that lives in me. Remind me daily Lord that this gift is designed to strengthen me as Your servant and help me not to live in fear, but to lead with the full Armor of God, serving You and Your kingdom on Earth.

In Christ's sweet and glorious name I pray, amen.

1 CHRONICLES 28:20 David also said to Solomon his son, "Be strong and courageous, and do the work. Do not be afraid or discouraged, for the Lord God, my God, is with you. He will not fail you or forsake you until all the work for the service of the temple of the Lord is finished."

JOSHUA 1:9 Have I not commanded you? Be strong and courageous. Do not be afraid; do not be discouraged, for the Lord your God will be with you wherever you go.

When my wife left the marriage, I was in "church limbo." I had been attending a church near my house, but had not rooted myself into that church community. I knew several of my close friends who were attending a mega-church in town, so I decided that I would visit that church, hoping to get some emotional support. When I arrived, I was very intimidated. I couldn't find a place to park and felt like this place was far too big for me. Despite my reluctance to stay, I kept driving around actually hoping I wouldn't find a place to park, so I could just go home and sulk.

Needless to say, I found a spot to park, grabbed my son and hurried inside not knowing what I was going to experience. The church service wasn't held in a typical sanctuary; it was an auditorium. Three thousand seats were screaming at me to run out the door and never come back. But as I walked through the doors entering the sanctuary I heard a beautiful voice singing a song about holding onto my Savior. Because the rawness of my broken heart was still fresh, I couldn't hold back my emotions. Crying, I found a place in the back of the sanctuary, sat down quickly, and hoped no one had noticed me. When the music ended, a tall, slender man stepped to the podium. It was if he looked straight at me and knew exactly what to say to speak life back into my broken soul. He preached on Joshua 1:9: "Have I not commanded you? Be strong and courageous. Do not be afraid; do not be discouraged, for the Lord your God will be with you wherever you go."

As I drove to church that morning, I had struggled with thoughts that God had done this evil thing to me, punishing me for the transgressions of my past. Somehow, I was getting exactly what I deserved. But the words that flowed out of the pastor's mouth weren't condemning words, but words of encouragement—words letting me know God was not against me, but was preparing me for something greater, even though I didn't understand at that point where I was heading. God was not punishing, He was preparing me to do His work, to accomplish His plan, to achieve His purpose. I left the church encouraged that God was going to use what had happened to me for His glory and that right now understanding the "why" didn't matter as much as just letting my spirit follow.

DAY 7 LETTING GO OF MY BROKENNESS

O Heavenly Father,

Help me, Lord, to make every step I take a closer walk to You. I ask for every opportunity to see our glorious Savior in others I need to serve. If I can lay down my own flesh at Your cross and take up the sword of the Spirit and embolden my faith, I know You can use me to heal those who are suffering around me. You are an Awesome God. Help to heal my own wounds so I'm not fixated on my flesh, but willing to serve You in fullness, wholeness and righteousness. As the days of this journey continue, I have learned that there is purpose and glory, even in suffering. It is found when human pride falls and a relationship with You arises. I walk across the bridge of my Savior into Your glorious arms. It is in that moment when I realize that You are comforting me because You also want me to comfort others. My purpose is to serve You; help me see how I can use this day to help those around me.

In Christ's name I pray, amen.

Romans 12:11 Never be lacking in zeal, but keep your spiritual fervor, serving the Lord.

Ephesians 6:16-18 In addition to all this, take up the shield of faith, with which you can extinguish all the flaming arrows of the evil one. Take the helmet of salvation and the sword of the Spirit, which is the word of God. And pray in the Spirit on all occasions with all kinds of prayers and requests. With this in mind, be alert and always keep on praying for all the Lord's people.

I wrote this prayer after attending one of the "Divorce Care" classes offered by my church. I began to understand, through my interaction with other members in the class, how God was using me to minister to others. Each class was an opportunity to serve God through the words I was writing and, in return, I could see that my strength and faith were growing more and more. Helping others around me, who were struggling with the same pain, to turn their hearts toward God for their own comfort and healing was healing my own wounds.

DAY 8 MY ATTITUDE IS CONTAGIOUS

O Heavenly Father,

Help me, Lord, to have an attitude that gives life to all I meet and shows the world that the Spirit of Your beautiful Son lives in me. As the daily challenges of life wear me down, I can get lost in myself and lose focus on the purpose of this day. As You have drawn me in and revealed the Holy Spirit who lives in me, I am starting to see there is nothing laid before me that is greater than the Spirit that lives in me. I can see with clarity that the greatest power I possess is the ability to show the world, through my actions and, most importantly, my attitude, that Christ lives in me. My attitude is contagious and has the power to change everyone around me. It is the most important thing I will carry with me on this journey in life. Lord, with all the power of Jesus that is in me, show the world by my attitude that there is nothing I cannot overcome with Your love leading the way. It is through my submission to Christ that I will not allow this broken world to change the spirit of the Gospel of Christ that dwells in me. Indeed, through His strength others will see the glorious richness of Your Son in me as my attitude changes their hearts and leads them on a path to discover who they are in Christ.

In Christ's name I pray, amen.

PHILIPPIANS 2:1-2 Therefore if you have any encouragement from being united with Christ, if any comfort from his love, if any common sharing in the Spirit, if any tenderness and compassion, then make my joy complete by being like-minded, having the same love, being one in spirit and of one mind.

1 John 1:7 But if we walk in the light, as he is in the light, we have fellowship with one another, and the blood of Jesus, his Son, purifies us from all sin.

One night when I was praying, I had fallen to my knees asking God to show me how to bring Him glory from my circumstances, and the prayer above is what my spirit was led to write. It made me wonder how does God really interact with this broken world? One way is through my attitude. It is my personal reflection of Jesus. It has an absolutely amazing ability to transform others around me. If you have never tried it, I suggest adopting a positive attitude and see how it influences those in your life. A loving, gracious attitude has the power to change someone's day.

We cannot change our circumstances, but we can change our perspective. I love a quote by Irving Berlin: "Life is ten percent what you make it and ninety percent how you take it." This quote and a song by Shawn McDonald led me to write, "There is nothing that comes before me that is greater than the power of Christ that is within me." What I am really saying here is that I believe in the victory of the Cross. It isn't a metaphor. The living breathing Spirit of God lives in me and through me; my attitude has the power to change lives, heal hearts, and paint a living picture of the Gospel on the world around me. It is more powerful than anything life can throw at me. When I show those in my life—even those who have hurt me—the Spirit of God through my attitude, the miracle of God's grace and healing shines brighter and the victory of the Cross is revealed through my actions.

Now, by surrendering to the Spirit of God, my attitude has power. As my own Savior has taught me, submitting to God allows Him to change lives through me, not by changing circumstances, but by allowing the world to see how an attitude of gratitude and grace brings alive the Gospel and reflects the healing power of Christ onto a broken world. This reflection is the rainbow after the storm. It shows the world through our own actions that the Spirit of Christ did not die on the Cross, but is alive and working in us.

10
Revealing My Weaknesses

DAY 9 PREPARING ME TO SERVE

O Heavenly Father,

I have learned that, through my weakness and suffering, You are preparing me with purpose to bring glory to You. In my weakness, I willingly give my heart to You and Your love covers over me. Through trust, I begin to submit to the direction of the Holy Spirit and each step I take is being led by You with purpose and direction. Slowly I realize that, even though I am wounded by the trials of life, I am gaining strength. I notice that as a result of my growing love for Jesus, the colors of life are brighter, more vivid, and a passion for life is emerging in me.

The painful tears that would not stop are replaced by gratitude that through all my mistakes, You never let go of me. Finally, in my total awareness of Your presence in me, I am transformed by Your love. Now I realize that I am nothing without You, but with You leading the way I can accomplish all things. Lord, I am so thankful that through this trial You have prepared me to bear fruit. I cry out to You Lord; I am ripe and ready to serve. Harvest me to bring glory to You and allow my life to serve Your divine purpose.

In Christ's name I pray, amen.

ISAIAH 41:10 [S]o do not fear, for I am with you; do not be dismayed, for I am your God. I will strengthen you and help you; I will uphold you with my righteous right hand.

When it seemed like my world had fallen apart, I was struggling with the idea that I thought God was going to protect me. I was trapped in the mindset that being a believer offered me some type of protection from the world around me. Somehow I was special and the bad things that happen in the world wouldn't happen to me. I can tell you from my experience: it is a rude awakening when you realize that the world you live in is a dangerous place and bad things will happen to you.

Many parts of scripture talk about God's protection, but I guess the real question is: how does God protect me? What I have come to believe is that God's protection is based on our dependence on Him. It's not a matter of protecting my home, my bank accounts, my relationships, all the stuff I own, or even my physical health; it is simply protecting my heart. My heart is the foundation of my faith and helps me determine how I choose to see my circumstances.

Being able to take each day as it is, allows me to experience both the good and bad in life. This allows God to use all circumstances for His purpose and His glory. The result is an internal peace. So that I can reveal my weaknesses, serve God's people, and draw closer to God's heart. When I started to wake up each day being able to take the day "as is", my perspective on life changed and so did the happiness each day brought me.

DAY 10 THE RAIN LEADS TO RAINBOWS

O Heavenly Father,

As I listen to the rain outside, the Holy Spirit reminds me how much I need the rain in my life that I may grow close to You. It is the rain that nourishes the grass and the trees and provides abundant life everywhere. Without the rain there would be no life and no beauty from the rainbows that blanket the sky after a thunderstorm.

As I look back on my life, I realize it is the dark, cloudy days of my life when I need You. Those are the times I feel vulnerable and let go of my pride and expose the innermost desires of my heart to You.

I know that You know my heart, and I am thankful to an awesome God who has not allowed me to fall away during the rainstorms in my life. Instead you have opened my eyes to Your amazing presence in me and showed me how the rain represents the times in my life when my heart is vulnerable. As I surrender myself to Your Spirit, my dependence on You grows more every day. This new Presence becomes a light and inner voice for me to follow, and I am now listening to You guide my steps. I now realize that it is the rain that nourishes me because it draws me closer to You. Without You I am nothing; but with You, no matter what I am facing, I will survive. Help me, Lord, in all my weakness as the rain falls around me, to continue to listen to You draw me ever closer to the Gift of You in me.

In Christ's name I pray, amen.

Zechariah 10:1 Ask the Lord for rain in the springtime; it is the Lord who sends the thunderstorms. He gives showers of rain to all people, and plants of the field to everyone.

> **Isaiah 30:23** He will also send you rain for the seed you sow in the ground and the food that comes from the land will be rich and plentiful. In that day your cattle will graze in broad meadows.

How ironic is it that it takes the worst things in life to show us the best things in ourselves. You never truly know what you're made of until life puts you to the test. It is easy to say, "Don't worry, you'll get through it." But what became my response every time someone said that to me was: "I don't want to get through it; I want to grow through it." If I just devote my energy to getting through it, I will not become a better man for it. I wanted to learn all that God desired for me to learn so I could glorify Him. Then the image of Jesus would shine through my circumstances. In that way, I would be a better man for having grown through the difficulty.

DAY 11 MY TRUE HAPPINESS IS IN YOU

O Heavenly Father,

As I awake today, Lord, I feel You tenderly pushing me toward a place in my life that has extraordinary possibilities. Your presence and closeness have revealed that for most of my life I have looked to others for my happiness. I realize that all along You have placed in me a desire to know You. My inability to find happiness from others has left me empty and has continually brought me back to You. Somewhere inside, I feel myself being drawn to You, seeking a closer and more complete relationship with my Creator. I know that my happiness must start here and grow out toward others, revealing not my dependence on them for happiness, but, instead, through Your reflection in me, that the world will see Your Son and I will radiate His joy toward them. It is this realization, that I am not dependent on the world for my joy but on Your gift of the Holy Spirit that touches the deepest parts of my heart. It brings me joy at the dawn of each day. Extraordinary possibilities will come the more I look to You for my happiness.

In Christ's sweet and holy name I pray, amen.

Lamentations 3:25 The LORD is good to those whose hope is in him, to the one who seeks him;

Hebrews 11:6 And without faith it is impossible to please God, because anyone who comes to him must believe that he exists and that he rewards those who earnestly seek him.

Psalm 13:3 Look on me and answer, Lord my God. Give light to my eyes, or I will sleep in death...

This prayer was simply life changing for me. It was when I understood that the world is not responsible for my happiness. When I connected to His Love Story, I found a joy the world could not provide me. Despite the sorrow and loss I was feeling, nothing separated me from His love, and I came alive in the middle of a life-changing tragedy. Each day knowing and feeling God was with me not only changed me, but it also changed my perspective. It gave me hope and helped me see that each day was more about Him and less about me. I started my day seeking Him instead of serving myself. It was amazing how a simple change of perspective brought a new life to me. I would encourage anyone who is struggling to seek opportunities to serve God. Document how your attitude changes as well as how it impacts others in your life.

DAY 12 PUTTING MY FEET IN THE WATER

O Heavenly Father,

I will praise You in the darkness and I will praise You when the sunlight radiates Your abundance. Every day You have drawn me closer through this trial. The Holy Spirit is beginning to reveal clarity to my day that was missing before You drew me near to You. Now You have placed the Jordan River in front of me and asked that I show my trust in You by putting my feet in the water. My trust is growing, O Lord, as You have carried me along this journey revealing Your presence at every turn. I am watching my faith grow by the silent call You have placed in my heart as the waters of the Jordan River have receded from my path. Thank You, Lord, for Your mercy and tenderness as You guide me on this journey to draw me close to Your Son. Thank You for Your Son Jesus and the passion You have placed in my heart that I may not only seek His presence but desire to submit to His will.
In Christ's name I pray, amen.

Psalm 28:6-9 Praise be to the Lord, for he has heard my cry for mercy. The Lord is my strength and my shield; my heart trusts in him, and he helps me. My heart leaps for joy, and with my song I praise him. The Lord is the strength of his people, a fortress of salvation for his anointed one.

DAY 13 LISTENING TO YOU

O Heavenly Father,

My pride is falling as I am letting go of the wounds of my past. The clarity of Your divine plan is unfolding as You are replacing hurts with healing. My heart is exploding with joy as I am now more aware of Your unfailing love for me. Your Word has taught me that You called me by my name and created me in Your own image, not for my pleasure but to serve an awesome God. You have, with tender mercy and compassion, given me salvation in our beloved Christ Jesus. You have offered me a lifelong companion in the Holy Spirit. Be patient as I am learning to seek His counsel. You have commanded me to lay down my selfish desires, take up the Cross and serve You. The joy I am beginning to feel as You tear down the walls of Jericho I built out of pride, selfishness and my personal agenda is showing me a life I have been missing. My heart is open to You Lord, and I ask with joyfulness that You continue to tear down the walls of pride and selfishness and teach me that through all circumstances I am here to serve You!

In Christ's name I pray, amen.

JOHN 3:16 For God so loved the world, that he gave his one and only Son, that whoever believes in him shall not perish but have eternal life.

PSALM 139: 1-24 You have searched me, Lord, and you know me. You know when I sit and when I rise; you perceive my thoughts from afar. You discern my going out and my lying down; you are familiar with all my ways. Before a word is on my tongue you, Lord, know it completely.

You hem me in behind and before, and you lay your hand upon me. Such knowledge is too wonderful for me, too lofty for me to attain. Where can I go from your Spirit? Where can I flee from your presence? If I go up to the heavens, you are there; if I make my bed in the depths, you are there. If I rise on the wings of the dawn, if I settle on the far side of the sea, even there your hand will guide me, your right hand will hold me fast. If I say, "Surely the darkness will hide me and the light become night around me," even the darkness will not be dark to you; the night will shine like the day, for darkness is as light to you.

For you created my inmost being; you knit me together in my mother's womb. I praise you because I am fearfully and wonderfully made; your works are wonderful, I know that full well. My frame was not hidden from you when I was made in the secret place, when I was woven together in the depths of the earth. Your eyes saw my unformed body; all the days ordained for me were written in your book before one of them came to be. How precious to me are your thoughts, God! How vast is the sum of them! Were I to count them, they would outnumber the grains of sand—when I awake, I am still with you.

If only you, God, would slay the wicked! Away from me, you who are bloodthirsty! They speak of you with evil intent; your adversaries misuse your name. Do I not hate those who hate you, Lord, and abhor those who are in rebellion against you? I have nothing but hatred for them; I count them my enemies. Search me, God, and know my heart; test me and know my anxious thoughts. See if there is any offensive way in me, and lead me in the way everlasting.

One of the biggest driving forces during this journey was my son. He was my motivation as I fought through the challenges of separation and divorce. Sadly though, before God laid this trial at my feet, teaching my son about Jesus was not a priority to me; it was my former wife's. But as my heart opened to God's Love Story, it became my passion to share with him the love my heart felt for Jesus. For the first time in my life, I desired to be the spiritual leader of my home and show him I was being led by the Holy Spirit. What amazed me along this journey was how God used people in my life to teach me what He desired for me to learn. Every day I prayed for God to protect my heart so I would not be jaded toward the possibility of reconciliation or, if it was not God's will for us to reconcile our marriage, then allowing my heart to be vulnerable again toward another woman. God answered my prayer through the sweet words of my child and showed me what God had been longing for me to learn. One of the darkest days of my recovery became one of the best days of my life.

One morning, while I was struggling with anger, my now five-year-old son realized that I was having a hard time. While we were driving to his grandparents, he said to me, "Daddy, guess what?" I replied, "Tell me, buddy." He said, "I love you like Jesus loves me." Hearing those sweet words come out of the mouth of a five-year-old transformed me. My mood changed completely as God literally reached out to me through the innocence of my son. As I looked at him through my rear view mirror, my eyes started tearing up. I realized my anger had changed to joy hearing the healing power of those words, "Jesus loves me." It showed me exactly what I needed to do to heal. I needed to love everyone in my life like Jesus loves me, and everyone meant everyone. This was the most defining moment of the year for me. God used my son to minister His Word to me, and reveal the healing presence of the Holy Spirit.

DAY 14 I AM YOUR CROWN OF JEWELS

O Heavenly Father,

The more my heart opens to Your glorious love for me, the more I realize how much I need You to guide every step I take. I know that my Savior suffered the Cross for me so that I may receive the gift of the Holy Spirit. I feel overwhelmed by the sacrifice You have made for me and unworthy of all that You have done to carry me on this journey to find Christ Jesus within myself. At the same time, my unworthiness gives way to abundant praise as I rejoice in the presence of Christ Jesus dwelling in my heart and leading me toward the will of my Maker. The closer I get to You, the more peace, acceptance, and glory my heart feels. I am Your crown of jewels made for only Your divine purpose. Carry me, O Lord, on the journey You have set forth for me so that I may bring glory to Your kingdom.

In Christ's name I pray, amen.

Proverbs 3:5-6 Trust in the LORD with all your heart and lean not on your own understanding; in all your ways submit to him, and he will make your paths straight.

DAY 15 BREAKING THE CHAINS IN ME

Oh Heavenly Father,

I am in awe of the miracle that You have placed in me. For so long I lived unaware of the magnificent life that has been with me since the moment I began to form in my mother's womb. Now this broken world has brought me to my knees and the darkness that rules it wants to push me away from Your light and lead me on a path of loneliness and isolation. As I have spent more and more time with You, the darkness of this broken world no longer has any power over my thoughts. You have raised me up out of the ashes, washed me clean of my sin, and made me aware of the power of Christ that lives in me. You have shown me Your greatness by Your victory over the grave and the darkness that rules the broken world. I am now able to cast away any thought that pushes me away from Your love. You have designed me to be closely connected to You and, as my awareness of Your presence in me grows, I am strengthened by Your transforming love, grace, and mercy.

I realize at last that I am not making it through this life, but You are making me as I am learning to surrender. Each day that I submit to You, I gain Your strength. You carry me on eagle's wings and give me peace with every step I take. I no longer feel like I am walking away from You, but through the power of submission, I am following Your love that lives in my heart. Thank you, Lord, for every step I have taken that has led me to You. No matter how difficult the path has been, I now can see that You are molding me through this glorious journey to find out who I am in Christ. I ask you,

Lord, with the power of Christ that lives in me, to pour forth Your Spirit so that the fountain of love I feel guiding my heart will never run dry. Please keep my feet moving in Your direction so my life is given in thankfulness to serve You.

In Christ's name I pray, amen.

Psalm 19:8 The precepts of the Lord are right, giving joy to the heart. The commands of the Lord are radiant, giving light to the eyes.

Isaiah 40:31 [B]ut those who hope in the Lord will renew their strength. They will soar on wings like eagles; they will run and not grow weary, they will walk and not be faint.

Raising children when you're divorced or separated is a difficult task, especially if either parent has been hurt emotionally. One of the many objectives of parenting is to help your children to acquire the knowledge to succeed in life. This includes their education, wellness, and spiritual life. In many ways, I view this objective as a war and within the war, there will be many battles. Sometimes you're going to need to lose a battle or two along the way in order to achieve the objective of winning the war. Like baseball when you have a runner on second and want to advance the runner to third, you sacrifice the batter by bunting and advancing the runner to third. You improve your position to score a run, but sacrifice an out to do so. There will be many times this is necessary in your relationship with your former spouse to raise your children. Sometimes being right isn't as important as doing right. Remember to focus on your objectives and realize that you can't control the other person. Letting that inner voice of reason overcome any obstacles means surrendering to the Holy Spirit which brings glory to God through your conflict.

I am fortunate to have rebuilt an amicable relationship with my former wife, but I could only achieve this because I was more concerned with the well-being of my son than I was with being right. Reading Isaiah 40:31 gave me insight.

I realized from my own experience of being raised in a broken home how easy it is for a child to get lost when parents don't communicate. I didn't want the circumstances of our divorce to make my son grow weary; I want him to be strong and face all his challenges with the strength God has given him. I want to be an example for him, to point his heart toward his faith to help him adjust to the mistakes I've made as a parent. I want to see him soar on eagle's wings and gain strength through his trials and not grow weary. Having a two-parent experience is critical to achieving this goal.

I would encourage all parents in similar situations to let go of the chains that are holding you back from communicating with your former partner. Help your children adjust to the mistakes that have been made. Breaking the chains will let God's love shine through all circumstances, allowing healing of broken hearts, broken promises, and broken homes.

DAY 16 MOLDING ME

Are you concerned about being a good man or good woman, or a godly man or godly woman?

O Heavenly Father,

I am, with each breath I take, learning that You are present at every fork in the road of my life. I have, at times of weakness, lost faith and trust in You, relying on myself and a broken world to judge my actions. I realize that the world around me does not care if I abide in Your word. I must trust where I am at every fork, knowing You are not only present, but in control of my steps if I submit to the truth found in Your Word. I cry out to You, Lord, with all the power that You have granted Jesus, that His blood transform my heart according to Your will. Lead me in the ways of a godly man so I may bring glory to You and be pleasing in Your eyes.

In Christ's name I pray, amen.

PSALM 31:5 Into your hands I commit my spirit; deliver me, Lord, my faithful God.

When you're hurting, it is so hard to avoid reacting to things that are happening around you. Learning to make time for God each day was critical in helping me seek His will in my circumstances. Making time for God helped me tune out the noise and tune in to His inner voice. Although I have never heard an audible voice, when I've spent quiet time in prayer asking God to lead my choices, the decisions I have made have always led toward grace and have produced healing. When I have relied only on myself to make decisions, the outcome was never the same.

DAY 17 MY HEART IS YOURS

O Heavenly Father,

You have placed before me a path that is filled with unimaginable twists, unexpected blessings, grace, joy and love. Every day my confidence is growing as You are romancing my heart. Your presence is everywhere during this difficult trial and my trust in You is growing strong. I am now beginning to see the lifelong love story with Jesus that You have scripted for my life. He is drawing me closer to You in the midst of my pain. I praise You, Lord, as I wait for You to guide my next step.

I am on my knees, Lord, arms stretched out and heart open, crying out for You to teach me to lead others and serve. Thank You, Lord, for not leaving me in a storm, for romancing my heart, for my lifelong love story with Jesus, and for the constant wind at my back nudging me in a direction that will bring glory to You, the Most High.

In Christ's glorious name I pray, amen.

Psalm 25:4-5 Show me your ways, Lord, teach me your paths. Guide me in your truth and teach me, for you are God my Savior, and my hope is in you all day long.

11
Finding My Joy

DAY 18 TRIALS ARE AN OPPORTUNITY TO GROW MY FAITH

O Heavenly Father,

Learning to find joy as You are molding me during life's trials is an exercise testing my faith and perseverance. This exercise seemed fruitless and difficult as I began the journey, but I continued to praise You even at times when my heart was not in it. Now, as You have opened my eyes to Your works in me, it has sustained me. Even between tears I lift my hands to You and offer all myself, as I know You are working miracles in me. I pray that You continue to strengthen my faith so I may persevere and allow others to see Your strength working in me. I ask You, with all the power You have given Jesus, to allow the Holy Spirit to continue shaping me through this trial in life so I may be fully transformed and bring glory to You. As I have grown close to and dependent on You, O Lord, give me the wisdom to see the purpose of each day. I understand now that I must lay aside my own pride to allow me to see the wisdom of my circumstances in order to serve You. Lord, may this day be all Yours to teach me Your grace, mercy, and love.

In Christ's Holy name I pray, amen.

James 1:2-5 Consider it pure joy, my brothers and sisters, whenever you face trials of many kinds, because you know that the testing of your faith produces perseverance. Let perseverance finish its work so that you may be mature and complete, not lacking anything. If any of you lacks wisdom, you should ask God, who gives generously to all without finding fault, and it will be given to you.

I believe most of us can say we have encountered one person in our lives that for some reason has transformed us in one way or another. Looking back on my life, it was a friend of mine who was diagnosed with a terminal cancer. When she received the news her cancer was incurable she immediately asked God for direction: "Okay God, you gave me cancer, now what?" For the next seven years she woke up every day with the desire to serve God through her cancer. It wasn't a negotiation with God in which she said: "Cure this cancer and I'll serve you." No, that wasn't her mantra; instead, her life verse was:

1 Thessalonians 5:16-18 Rejoice always, pray continually, give thanks in all circumstances; for this is God's will for you in Christ Jesus.

The night I wrote my prayer thanking God on page 17, I couldn't stop thinking about her. I couldn't stop thinking about how she served God through some of life's most difficult circumstances. In fact, one of my favorite stories about her indomitable spirit occurred when she had become gravely ill from one of the cancer treatments. I was part of a men's Bible study group that included her husband. I had received emails that she was in the hospital and not doing well. Apparently the treatment she was receiving to fight the cancer had compromised her immune system and it was touch and go all week. Our Bible study group met on Wednesday nights and we spent a good deal of our time praying for her. The next day my cell phone rang and the number was hers. I started to panic thinking the worst. When I reluctantly answered the call, her bubbly, bright voice echoed through the phone: "Hey Michael, I just wanted to let you know I am throwing a surprise fortieth birthday party for my husband Saturday, can you make it?" Blown away, I asked her: "Aren't you supposed to be sick?" Her reply was typical: "I don't have time for that right now—this is way more important." Wow, what an amazing soul is all I could think about.

Attending her funeral service several years later, about two thousand people were packed into a tiny church. I believe no one left that church feeling sorry for this amazing woman who died at the early age of thirty-nine, but wishing that their lives looked more like hers. This included yours truly. Her impact on me spiritually was a big reason I turned toward God when my heart was broken. She was a living example of what it looks like to take tragic news and turn it into an opportunity to serve God.

DAY 19 THE TRANSFORMING POWER OF GRACE

O Heavenly Father,

As my heart is healing, I can feel the warmth of Your light shining on me. This blanket of love is becoming my shelter, my rock. I cannot believe I spent so much of my life oblivious to Your presence in me. This journey to find You, Heavenly Father, is full of Your wisdom, as You have used my circumstances to bring me closer in my relationship to You. It is Your grace, love and wisdom found in Jesus that have transformed my soul and made me want to be a Christ-centered, godly man. You have shown me that, in order to achieve this goal, my actions and my words must walk hand in hand with Your word. Help me, Lord, to be a godly man in my words and my actions. As the Holy Spirit has begun to take control of me and I have started to submit to His presence, I have witnessed how my actions of grace toward my circumstances have impacted others all around me. I know, Lord, that this is how I bring glory to You and demonstrate to the world around me that Christ is present and working in me. Continue, Lord, to use me and my circumstances so the world can see the beauty of Your precious Son alive and working in me.

In Christ's name I pray, amen.

GALATIANS 2:20 I have been crucified with Christ and I no longer live, but Christ lives in me. The life I now live in the body, I live by faith in the Son of God, who loved me and gave himself for me.

DAY 20 GIVING MY WORRIES TO YOU

O Heavenly Father,

Help me lay at Your feet the worries of my day. I am consumed with the worldly idea that I can control the outcome of my day and serve You according to Your will at the same time. How foolish am I when my mind is deceived by these thoughts of control. You have been working on me on this issue, but I am stubborn. Release me from the deception that I am in control of my life. Help me understand I am here to serve You and must submit my worries and lack of patience to a God who knows the beginning and end of all things. Remind me that You loved me enough to send Jesus in place of my sinful self. I know to You, I am one of your glorious creations, but I allow the worries of my day to get in the way of Your perfect will. O Lord, I want to give You my best, and allow you to work your miracles through me. Lord, help me get out of the way so all that is good within me can be used to serve You and Your Kingdom here on earth.

In Christ's name I pray, amen.

PHILIPPIANS 4:6-7 Do not be anxious about anything, but in every situation, by prayer and petition, with thanksgiving, present your requests to God. And the peace of God, which transcends all understanding, will guard your hearts and your minds in Christ Jesus.

DAY 21 BE STILL; YOU ARE MY JOY

O Heavenly Father,

I am thankful that You have not allowed me to rob myself of the love You specifically placed in my heart as a result of the bitterness of life's circumstances. You have called on me to find joy in all of life's trials and tribulations. I praise You Lord for Your patience as my faith is growing. I realize now the world expects me to react to life's circumstances, but you desire that I keep still and listen to the Holy Spirit guide me and my reactions. I know Your Word is true, that You will shape the mountains of my life, but I must be still and allow Your Love Story inside me to guide each step I take. I know that Holy Spirit is Your gift of love to be my guide and constant companion. This blessing has begun to shape every part of me, and I am clinging to Your love as my heart is continuing to heal and grow. I know this love allows me to serve You and share the love of Christ with others. I ask You, Lord, with the power and presence You have given the Holy Spirit, to continue to protect the love in my heart, allowing myself to be vulnerable and share it openly with others. Help me, Lord, to wait patiently for Your guidance and listen to Your voice to lead my steps. The love You have placed in my heart is precious. I want to share it with those close to me so that I can be the example that You intended me to be. I am so blessed by the joy Your love has brought me; sharing it with others has become my reason for living.

In Christ's name I pray, amen.

Proverbs 16:9 In their hearts humans plan their course, but the Lord establishes their steps.

Psalm 37:23 The Lord makes firm the steps of the one who delights in him.

When I was spending an afternoon with my brother-in-law, the pastor, he asked me, “How are you spending time with God every day?” I told him that I had been reading my Bible and several devotionals. He repeated his question, “How are you spending time with God?” Confused, I responded with the same answer. He then asked me if I had one hundred books about my wife and read them all, but never spent any real time with her, would I really know her? I then understood his point. He suggested that I find a quiet place to sit and spend time with God every day. When you actually spend time with Him and seek His inner voice, He will reveal to you a great many things. You will learn to listen to His guidance and He will lead you always toward grace. My brother-in-law’s advice helped me redefine what it meant to spend time with God every day. It was amazing how much peace I received and the closeness I felt when I made this a priority in my life.

DAY 22 YOUR LOVE IS SHAPING MY FUTURE

O Heavenly Father,

There is no way my heart can understand Your amazing love for me. I cannot wrap my thoughts around the sacrifice You made for me and the unconditional love of Jesus. There is so much wisdom found in all that Jesus represents to the world that I am left at a loss for words. As I reflect on how Christ has changed me, I realize that my capacity to love is growing and the Holy Spirit is beginning to direct my steps. Although I am experiencing a difficult time in my life, You have taken hold of my spirit. You show me how much You love me by the constant blessings You have poured out on me in the middle of this storm. I praise You, Lord, for opening my heart to You as the rain falls on me, shaping my future and creating a longing to serve You. I pray, Lord, that You use me and my circumstances to inspire others who are also struggling, and show them that You are the answer to all their troubles.

In Christ's name I pray, amen.

2 Corinthians 13:14 May the grace of the Lord Jesus Christ, and the love of God, and the fellowship of the Holy Spirit be with you all.

Ephesians 1:3 Praise be to the God and Father of our Lord Jesus Christ, who has blessed us in the heavenly realms with every spiritual blessing in Christ.

DAY 23 I AM WEAK, BUT YOU ARE STRONG

O Heavenly Father,

I am constantly stumbling over myself in trying to find You. Although You have placed a beacon in my heart, I still find it so difficult, in the midst of this cluttered life, to serve You when I know I'm called to do so. Strengthen the power of Your signal calling me to You, O Lord. You have carried me through this storm and I am overwhelmed by Your grace as I continue to fall short of Your glory. Thank You, Lord, for holding onto me when my grip weakens and for not allowing me to slip away from Your loving arms. Your persistence is carving a love for Christ deep in my heart. I am seeing now with more clarity Your love story for me as it plays out in the midst of my daily battles. Even though I am weak, He is strong, and His love for me is intensifying my desire to seek Your will first in all things.

In Christ's name I pray, amen.

2 Thessalonians 3:5 May the Lord direct your hearts into God's love and Christ's perseverance.

Hebrews 12:1 Therefore, since we are surrounded by such a great cloud of witnesses, let us throw off everything that hinders and the sin that so easily entangles. And let us run with perseverance the race marked out for us[.]

2 Corinthians 12:9-10 But he said to me, "My grace is sufficient for you, for my power is made perfect in weakness." Therefore I will boast all the more gladly about my weaknesses, so that Christ's power may rest on me.

That is why, for Christ's sake, I delight in weaknesses, in insults, in hardships, in persecutions, in difficulties. For when I am weak, then I am strong.

DAY 24 IN YOU, I HAVE NO FEAR

O Heavenly Father,

Throughout Your Word You repeatedly tell me, "Do not fear." As my faith has grown, You have carried me along this glorious journey to find You resting in the depths of my heart. I praise You for every tear I have shed and every time I have fallen to my knees and found You there to pick me up. My fear about the future and not following Your divine plans for my life are nothing more than my own insecurities and lack of trust in You. Thank You, for revealing to me that, the more I become dependent on You and Your Word, the more peace I receive about my future as I allow You to direct my thoughts and guide my steps. I feel my heart growing every day, expanding outward toward others who long to experience the love of Jesus. Lord, I will no longer fear about my future. I lay at Your feet all my hopes and all my dreams. I know that You have a divine purpose for my life that is beyond my understanding. As I seek You first in all things, I know that You will open my heart to Your wisdom and blanket me with Your peace. Help me, Lord, to start each day consumed with the knowledge that You are the beginning and the end. If I meditate on the idea that I am here to be close to You, then the purpose of each day is to be drawn into the Love Story You've placed in me. There is no fear in Your perfect love for me. May that always be my peace.

In Christ's name I pray, amen.

Psalm 27:1 The Lord is my light and my salvation—whom shall I fear? The Lord is the stronghold of my life—of whom shall I be afraid?

> **1 Chronicles 28:20** David also said to Solomon his son, "Be strong and courageous, and do the work. Do not be afraid or discouraged, for the Lord God, my God, is with you. He will not fail you or forsake you until all the work for the service of the temple of the Lord is finished."

One of the many devastating outcomes of divorce and separation is the financial challenge that occurs due to loss or division of income. There is a great deal of fear when debt piles up, resulting in the possibility of losing your home and or bankruptcy. This reality hit me hard when my wife left. After reading Dave Ramsey's "Total Money Makeover," I followed his advice and refinanced my home mortgage from a thirty-year to a fifteen-year loan right before the separation. This raised my monthly mortgage payment substantially and made it almost impossible for me to make the payment on one income. Due to various lending restrictions, I was not able to refinance my mortgage loan again for six more months. My monthly financial obligations made it difficult to see how I was going to make it. Something was going to have to give. Even though I trimmed my budget to the bone and cut out my life insurance, I was still coming up short each month. One of my close friends suggested that I stop tithing until my financial situation improved, but I just couldn't do it. Even with feelings that God betrayed me, I felt I needed to stay faithful and trust that somehow things would work out.

About three weeks later, I posted on Facebook my prayer thanking God. One of my wife's best friends saw the prayer and thought something had happened to our son. He reached out to me, inquiring about the prayer. I didn't reply because I felt that the news about our separation needed to come from my wife. The next time I saw her, I let her know that her friend had reached out to me. I suggested she call him to let him know what had happened. Several weeks later, while I was sitting at my computer writing a prayer, he sent me a message asking if he could call me. After I agreed, he called immediately. I was shocked to find out that my wife had not contacted him. After I explained what happened, he asked how he could help. I told him that I was struggling with anger and needed prayer support. It happened that he had been teaching divinity courses at a Christian school and had articles dealing with the issue of anger and resentment. He said he would be in town the next day and would drop them by my office. He then inquired about my financial situation. I explained that I was making it, but things were very tight. He explained that he and his wife wanted to help me in some way and asked me the amount of my mortgage payment. He told me they would pray about it and let me know how they would help.

The next day he stopped by and left the articles on my desk while I was out of my office. When I returned, I was very surprised to find that he and his wife had written a check in the amount of my mortgage payment and left it attached to the articles. I immediately started to cry, overwhelmed by his generosity. Later that afternoon, another friend paid the daycare bill for my son. Then, a week later, two of my clients handed me checks to help me through the financial challenges the separation has caused. All of the financial help I received was just enough. It was as if God knew exactly how much money I needed to get me through. Once I refinanced my mortgage and my son entered kindergarten, I was finally able to handle my financial obligations. This was one of the times I really put God to the test—I stayed faithful in my own giving and God showed me that I can't out give Him.

> **Malachi 3:10** "Bring the whole tithe into the storehouse, that there may be food in my house. Test me in this," says the Lord Almighty, "and see if I will not throw open the floodgates of heaven and pour out so much blessing that there will not be room enough to store it."

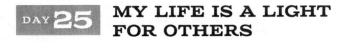

DAY 25 MY LIFE IS A LIGHT FOR OTHERS

O Heavenly Father,

You light the way by the glorious life that lives in me. Today is not just another day; it is an opportunity to bring glory to You. In order to focus on the day before me, I give You the burdens of my heart, because You are the author of my life and have already scripted the beginning and end of this wonderful journey to find You. As I have begun this spiritual awakening, trust has been an essential part of serving You. I know it is Your divine purpose to breathe life into our hearts and light the way for all who are in need.

I ask You, Lord, to reveal the gifts You have created in me. You have designed me to bring glory to You by helping others in the areas You have equipped me to serve You. Light the way each day for me to use these gifts to serve the Gospel of Christ that lives in my heart. Keep the light of my heart lit so the reflection of Christ radiates outwardly, allowing those in my life to see Your reflection in me. Strengthen my walk that I might serve You more. I ask You, Lord, with all the power You have given the Holy Spirit, to use my life as a light for others to see the living Gospel in me.

In Christ's glorious name I pray, amen.

1 Peter 4:10 Each of you should use whatever gift you have received to serve others, as faithful stewards of God's grace in its various forms.

DAY 26 HOLDING ON TO ME

O Heavenly Father,

You carried me into the valley of darkness and revealed the light of Your presence in me. Now, with every step I take, my life has a renewed purpose. Even in the midst of my own shame, You transformed my broken heart and I will never be the same. Your love for me is beyond my understanding, but as You write on my heart the path to You, my ability to love increases every day. You have made me anew and I find myself seeking You first in all my circumstances. The anxiety I experienced when I approached the day is gone, and I am finding strength knowing that You are not only with me, but in control because I have given each day to You. Instead of worrying about the day, I seek Your wisdom in all circumstances and know You are holding me in the palm of Your hand. Jeremiah 29:11-13 says; "For I know the plans I have for you," declares the LORD, "plans to prosper you and not to harm you, plans to give you hope and a future." Then you will call on me and come and pray to me, and I will listen to you. You will seek me and find me when you seek me with all your heart."

I find so much comfort daily as I sit and listen to Your inner voice speak these words to me. Lord, I give this day to You to bring prosperity to Your kingdom and spread the Gospel of Christ You have placed in my heart. Thank You for the valley of darkness that led me to You!

In Christ's name I pray, amen.

I was inspired to compile my prayers into this journal by several members of my Divorce Care class. Often I would read prayers I had written dealing with issues we were covering in class. After the sessions were over, members of the class would tell me that what I had written spoke to them or helped them see a different perspective in the struggles they were having. Either in person or through email, they told me that what I had written was encouraging and inspirational.

One member of the class had a wife who left him after twenty-nine years of marriage for her college boyfriend. She was not a Christian, and over the years of their marriage had pulled him away from his faith. During one of the classes, I read my "Dear Jesus" prayer on page 24 that I had written asking Jesus why He had given His life for me. After class, he came up and asked me to help him find Jesus again. I was taken aback that my prayer had encouraged him to seek out his faith again. The feedback I gave to him then was very simple, and I still feel the same way I did then. I told him, "You don't need me to find Jesus; you simply need to get yourself out of the way and listen. He is there and always has been."

So, the next session I gave him a copy of *Mere Christianity* by C.S. Lewis. At each subsequent class he would talk with me about the struggles he was having in finding his faith again. I would simply tell him that getting pride out of the way is a process. He told me that until he could find his faith again, he was going to fake it until he'd make it. About a month later, he informed the class that he had given his life to Christ at church that previous Sunday. I was overwhelmed with joy that, through my pain, I had written something that had moved someone else who was hurting to find Jesus. This for me was another piece of the puzzle as I started to understand how God uses us to move the Gospel and share the healing power of Christ through the trials we endure and overcome.

DAY 27 HELP ME MOVE MOUNTAINS

O Heavenly Father,

The more You draw me close, the more I am amazed by You and Your grace. I am the reason You sent Your glorious son to die on the Cross, yet You still show me mercy as You have carried me through the trials of life. My faith and love for You is growing more and more every day as the reality and image of the Cross is imprinted on my heart. Now that You have awakened me, I am alive. You have opened my heart to know Jesus and moved me toward a place where I can hear His gentle whisper directing my thoughts. You have transformed me by the trials of life and prepared me to seek and find You as You reach down to hold me during my weakest moments. I have been able to persevere through it all because You have gone before me and prepared my heart to endure. It is only by Your amazing grace that I am not only still here, but thriving. In the midst of pain, the Holy Spirit has captivated my heart and romanced my soul, as I openly gave my day to You.

I am finding great strength moving in a direction that allows me to serve You. I am deeply thankful that You have protected my heart. I have an overwhelming sense of gratitude as I begin to see Your divine plans for my life unfold. You did not create me to sit still, but to be like a powerful wind spreading the Gospel of Christ that lives in me. I ask You, Lord, with the awesome power of Christ You have printed on my heart, that everyone You have placed in my life will be able to see the reflection of Jesus through my thoughts and my actions. Lord, continue to grow my faith so I may remove the mountains of anger, resentment, bitterness, unworthiness, and unwillingness to forgive, so others may see that Your glorious Son lives in me. May the purpose of all my words and actions move their spirits and open their hearts to the beautiful gift of Your Son that lives within them.

In Christ's name I pray, amen.

2 Peter 1:2 May God give you more and more grace and peace as you grow in your knowledge of God and Jesus our Lord.

Matthew 17:20 "You don't have enough faith," Jesus told them. "I tell you the truth, if you had faith even as small as a mustard seed, you could say to this mountain, 'Move from here to there,' and it would move. Nothing would be impossible."

DAY 28 MY HEART OVERFLOWS

O Heavenly Father,

It is Your radiant light that allows me to see the world around me with clarity and passion. My heart is an open well into which You have poured the Holy Spirit. Now, I have placed my hopes and dreams on You, and You have not forsaken me in my storm. I can only praise You as You unveil each day with blessings that are overflowing with Your love and compassion. Now I have learned, in the midst of life's storms, that I must first seek Your presence, trust that You have a divine plan to bring glory to You, and listen for Your gentle voice to lead me in that direction. Lord, I can feel You all around me. You have given me peace in the name of Jesus and I thank You, Heavenly Father, for filling my well with the spirit of Christ and leading my heart closer to You. My heart overflows with Your love and abundance.

In Christ's name I pray, amen.

Titus 3:5 He saved us, not because of the righteous things we had done, but because of His mercy. He saved us through the washing of rebirth and renewal by the Holy Spirit...

John 14:26 But the Advocate, the Holy Spirit, whom the Father will send in my name, will teach you all things and will remind you of everything I have said to you.

DAY 29 YOUR MIRACLES ARE EVERYWHERE

O Heavenly Father,

Your endless miracles are all around me. I have spent my life looking to find You in a miracle like the parting of the Red Sea and now I realize You were right in front of me all the time. O how blind and lost I have been on this journey! Now, like a powerful wind, I feel Your awesome power moving my feet toward You. I cannot stop this pilgrimage You have laid out before me. My heart is opening wider, as Your voice is calling to me. My desire to be obedient is growing, which is allowing me to see Your abundant miracles all around me. When my eyes and heart are fixed on Jesus, I can see His love being expressed everywhere. Even in the midst of my own trials, Lord, You are at constant work in my life and I praise You! With all the power of Jesus' blood, I humbly ask You, Lord, to increase the intensity of the storm You are using to transform me. Allow me to seek not only Your will, but to acknowledge every miracle found in Jesus so I may live in constant praise to You regardless of where I am on my journey.

In Christ's name I pray, amen.

Exodus 14:16 Raise your staff and stretch out your hand over the sea to divide the water so that the Israelites can go through the sea on dry ground.

Psalm 16:11 You make known to me the path of life; you will fill me with joy in your presence, with eternal pleasures at your right hand.

This prayer was my miracle healer. I wrote it when I realized that praying was not about changing my circumstances; it was about changing my perspective. It was the moment I learned to surrender all of myself to God and trust Him. I kept thinking that God was going to bring my wife back and our marriage would be restored. That was going to be my miracle, my parting of the Red Sea. However, the miracle wasn't looking outward, it was looking inward. It was surrendering myself to the Spirit of God and letting His work be done through me.

When I spent time praying to God about this, I realized how often we get caught up looking for God to perform miracles when all along the miracle isn't on the outside, it's what happens to us on the inside when we surrender ourselves to Him. Surrendering completely lets God do His work and that's when real miracles can happen.

Some may criticize the idea that this is a real miracle, but I disagree. When you look around and see the pain we bring on ourselves trying to control the world around us, you can appreciate the impossible task we set for ourselves. But, when we surrender ourselves to the will of God, real miracles can happen right before our eyes. I know we are looking for miraculous signs to prove God exists. To me, He is not found there. He is found when we surrender ourselves to Him and watch the miracle of healing happen in our relationships, our children, our families, and our communities. You don't need to survive being struck by lighting in order to find God; you just need to get out of the way. Putting aside your pride and sparing the innocent heart of your children is a miraculous healing. Putting your children's feelings first, as Christ put you first, is a miraculous healing. It is a healing of your pride that allows God to touch your heart and interact with the world around us. If that isn't a miracle, then I don't know what is.

12
God, I Trust You

DAY 30 THE LIFE THAT LIVES IN ME

O Heavenly Father,

Why do I allow myself to be robbed of the joyful life you have planned for me? The miracle of You living in me should be a constant reminder of Your great purpose for my life. Daily, Lord, I struggle with the idea that I deserve to live the abundant life that You have offered me through our precious Jesus. Why do I continue to look for approval from this broken world around me and not focus entirely on Your miracle in me. Please help me, Father. Why do I steal Your joyful life that lives in me?

The response I received:

"O, my child, the answer to your question is already written on your heart. You are simply not focusing on My presence that I left with you the moment you embraced My Son as your Savior. You must be still and listen to Me speaking to your heart. When My Son paid a ransom for you by carrying every burden of yours to the Cross, He left behind His Spirit to live in you. You only have to submit to His presence and a joyful life is awaiting you. If you spend time with Me, I will awaken you to the power and presence of Me that I placed in your heart. You must be willing to lay down your pride so I can connect your spirit with Mine and then I will breath life into all I bring before you. This is the beginning of a joyful and abundant life, which

is simply the realization that this life is not about you. You are not here to tell your story. I placed you here and prepared for you an opportunity to experience Me through your trials so you will tell My Love Story. You must always remember any thought that separates you from the idea that I designed you to live a life that is life-giving, does not come from Me. I am here to cast out the darkness that has taken hold of this broken world with a passion to destroy the miracle of Me in you. Be still and know that the greatest power of the universe lives in you. Listen to the wisdom of My love that I gave to you in My Son and rest in Me knowing that joyfulness is a gift that comes from realizing this presence in You. Every thought you have that comes from Me brings you closer to the purpose I have for you. You are my miracle in thought and action as My Son lives through you. I love you, my child, and you will find every gift that I have placed in You to be a part of My purpose to bring you closer to Me. You are talented because I gave you talent. You are beautiful because I created you. You are My miracle because I live in you. I made you to serve My Kingdom."

ROMANS 8:11 And if the Spirit of him who raised Jesus from the dead is living in you, he who raised Christ from the dead will also give life to your mortal bodies because of his Spirit who lives in you.

When I wrote this prayer, I was struggling deeply. This was part of my roller coaster ride of emotions that haunted me daily. Spiritually I was getting to a good place, but emotionally I still had so many questions racing through my mind. About four months after our separation, my father and step-mother took my son and me to Disney World. It was so difficult walking around Disney watching families having so much fun together. I couldn't fight off the questions that kept haunting me: "Why did this have to happen to me?" "What does it take to make a family work?" I thought I had been doing all the right things. I was respectful and faithful to my wife, working hard for our family and business, financially responsible and personally responsible. I thought I spent time understanding her. How could I have missed the obvious signs that she was unhappy? What was missing in my marriage? Seeing thousands of families happy and enjoying the Disney experience together made the trip a real challenge for me.

On the final night of the trip, we were enjoying the nighttime fireworks show at the Magic Kingdom. Holding my son in my arms, I couldn't help breaking down emotionally. I told my son that they were "happy" tears, but, in reality, I was deeply hurting inside, feeling like a total failure as a husband. In truth, I was a failure as a husband. I had failed to let God lead my marriage. Shortly after returning from the Disney trip, I wrote the "Marriage Prayer." It is the final prayer in this journal. It reflects all that God has taught me about the miracle of marriage and all that he revealed to me about what my marriage had been missing—God.

DAY 31 SEEING YOUR SCARS IN ME

O Heavenly Father,

Every day I want to look at my hands and see the scars of my Savior. I want to be reminded of His sacrifice so I can live in constant praise. At times, Lord, when life is not going according to my plan, I find it difficult to praise You. When I live seeking to please myself, I fail every time to see Your wisdom in my circumstances. When I am lost in myself, remind me to look at my hands and feel the Holy Spirit guide me back to the love of the Cross. Time is a precious healing gift and I know I cannot rush through the lessons life has presented to me. Help me see the opportunities You have given me to learn more so I can be closer to You. Every time life is a struggle, nudge me to look down at my hands and praise You in all of life's circumstances so that others may see in me the magnificent gift of Jesus.

In Christ's name I pray, amen.

JOHN 20:24-26 Now Thomas (also known as Didymus), one of the Twelve, was not with the disciples when Jesus came. So the other disciples told him, "We have seen the Lord!" But he said to them, "Unless I see the nail marks in his hands and put my finger where the nails were, and put my hand into his side, I will not believe." A week later his disciples were in the house again and Thomas was with them. Though the doors were locked, Jesus came and stood among them and said, "Peace be with you!"

DAY 32 STANDING FIRM

O Heavenly Father,

I can feel Your gentle hands lifting my chin and Your voice calling me to keep my head up so I can show the world that You are in me. I am now learning that the courage to move forward in a storm is not the absence of fear, but the presence of my growing faith in You. You have lifted me up when my heart and soul were down and carried me along this journey by revealing Your glorious presence to me. You have not forsaken me in this storm. I praise You for not hardening my heart, but opening it up and pouring in the Holy Spirit. I am standing firm in You, O Lord, and feel my strength growing as You are working Your miracles in me. I feel so blessed knowing You are with me every step I take and ask, Lord, with all the power You have granted the Holy Spirit, that You continue to strengthen my faith so I can walk on water with You.

In Christ's name I pray, amen.

1 Thessalonians 3:8 For now we really live, since you are standing firm in the Lord.

Ephesians 6:10-17 Finally, be strong in the Lord and in his mighty power. Put on the full armor of God, so that you can take your stand against the devil's schemes. For our struggle is not against flesh and blood, but against the rulers, against the authorities, against the powers of this dark world and against the spiritual forces of evil in the heavenly realms. Therefore put on the full armor of God, so that when the day of evil comes, you may be able to stand your ground, and after you have done everything, to stand.

> Stand firm then, with the belt of truth buckled around your waist, with the breastplate of righteousness in place, and with your feet fitted with the readiness that comes from the gospel of peace. In addition to all this, take up the shield of faith, with which you can extinguish all the flaming arrows of the evil one. Take the helmet of salvation and the sword of the Spirit, which is the word of God.

This prayer reflected how important it was for me to focus on the Holy Spirit every day. It was a reminder that life is going to be hard and will want to pull me away from my faith, but these moments are when I need to stand firm in my love and belief in God and seek His guidance. When I keep my focus on God and not let worldly troubles distract me, I can feel Him smile as His love and joy washes over me. These are usually the difficult times, but as my faith has grown, I feel nothing can penetrate God's love. That is why for me, putting on the armor of God daily is so important. It keeps me from being caught off guard, allowing wounds from our failed marriage to hurt my son. It is my tight rope, and I cling to the Amour of God for guidance every day.

DAY 33 AMAZING LOVE

O Heavenly Father,

There is no way my heart can understand Your amazing love. I cannot comprehend the sacrifice You made for me and the unconditional love of Jesus. There is so much wisdom found in all that Jesus represents to the world that I am left at a loss for words. As I reflect on how Christ has changed me, I realize my capacity to love others is growing and the presence of the Holy Spirit is directing my steps. Although life is a constant struggle, You have taken hold of my spirit and shown me how much You love me through the constant blessings You have poured out on me during the storms in my life. As I look back, I realize now that it has taken this difficult journey not just to find You, but to be willing to offer my spirit to You. That offer has allowed me to experience the intimate joy of loving You without my own walls of pride. I praise You, Lord, for opening my heart to You. You are nourishing my soul as the rain washes way my pride, allowing you to shape my future. This is creating a longing to serve You. I pray, Lord, that You use me and my circumstances to inspire others who are struggling along their own journeys and to help them look to You for their healing.

In Christ's name I pray, amen.

Deuteronomy 4:29-31 But if from there you seek the Lord your God, you will find him if you seek him with all your heart and with all your soul. When you are in distress and all these things have happened to you, then in later days you will return to the Lord your God and obey him. For the Lord your God is a merciful God; he will not abandon

> or destroy you or forget the covenant with your ancestors, which he confirmed to them by oath.

Why does God allow us suffer when He has the power to stop it? In one sense, this is a deeply theological question that I don't feel qualified to answer. However, in another sense, it is a deeply emotional question with which I have had to wrestle. Because I am left to experience the world as it is, I have to draw my own conclusions when I'm left hurting and alone. From a glance, the world we live in is an amazing place. One can use literally every adjective to describe its glory and beauty, yet it is dangerous. Because it is constantly changing, we have to be willing to take the good with the bad, the night and the day, the sun and the rain, and life and death. It is all part of an amazing design leaving us with so many unanswerable questions. For myself, I can only draw my conclusions based on my own limited knowledge and experiences.

When I take a step back and analyze the difficult question of why I am left by a loving God to suffer, I can only conclude that it is because He wants to draw me closer to Him. When times are good, have I ever really reached out to God in need? It seems the only times I have been drawn to God is when I need Him. It is a moment of clarity when the walls of Jericho tumble down and through my surrender, God touches me. I can't imagine I would have experienced God on a hilltop; it was in the valley where I found Him. It was a point in my existence that was my darkest moment, when I willing to let go of myself and believe that He is more than a word in a book. What I experienced wasn't a metaphor or moment of weakness. I have no proof in human terms, but how can you prove what you feel? In the valley of my life, I felt God's love touch me in such a way that I will never be the same man again. It fundamentally changed me and how I look at the world. What I experienced gave me more than hope for tomorrow; it gave me an internal joy. No longer could I focus on the wrongs committed against me; I was too thankful for the grace and mercy God showed me as well as the realization of the gift of the Holy Spirit.

Some might think it cruel to say that a loving God would let me suffer in order to draw me near to Him, but I disagree. Often our wisdom comes through suffering and mistakes. I believe that, if most of us were truly honest with ourselves, we would conclude that we've learned the most about our self through suffering. Suffering helps us gain a deeper understanding of our limitations, shows us our need for compassion, and strips the soul of its pride, allowing God an opportunity to touch us. It is when the world defeats our pride and we surrender to God.

Finding myself in the valley was my opportunity to experience God's love. He was the little light in my darkness giving me hope and direction. Just knowing He was there was peaceful. If you're asking yourself how I knew He was there, my answer is: I could feel Him. What I felt was something I cannot fully explain, but if you can imagine feeling totally complete, a wholeness filling every gap the world has left behind, you would understand. I wouldn't change a single tear I've shed because of what I have learned and, most importantly, what I have experienced. I am truly thankful that God, who had the power to stop it, chose to let it happen so that now I know His amazing love for me.

DAY 34 DEFINING MY CIRCUMSTANCES

O Heavenly Father,

The more You are in me, the more I realize that I am called to show the world the gift of the Holy Spirit despite my circumstances. I know, when I lay aside my own pride and allow You to live through me, I am not affected by my circumstances or the actions of others. Instead, I am able to embrace them all with your love. Therefore it is not my circumstances that define me, but You who defines my circumstances. When I am able show the world around me how You live through me, I come alive. That is how I am able to affect others You have placed in my life, by showing them Your love and compassion shining through me into a broken world. I have been made a "new" person through the trials along this journey You have set before me. Without hesitation, I fall on my knees, hands stretched out to You, praising You for the storms that have opened the flood gates to Your heart. I am Yours and You are mine. I want Your hands to mold me into the miracle You created me to be so I may bring glory to You, my precious Lord.

In Christ's Holy name I pray, amen.

JAMES 4:10 Humble yourselves before the Lord, and he will lift you up.

EPHESIANS 2:9 [N]ot by works, so that no one can boast.

There were many times in my journey when my pride wanted to react, letting all the hurt out. But when those moments occurred, I would say to myself, "Michael, stand firm, don't react to this!" One of the more difficult moments came when my son didn't want to leave his mother's apartment and told me he was mad at me because I didn't let her sleep at the house anymore. This was especially hurtful because at this point none of this had been my choice. But he was five-years-old and not capable of understanding the complexity of what was happening. He simply wanted to express his feelings, so I let him. I told my son that it was okay for him to be mad at me and he had every right to feel the way he was feeling. This was not the way that God had designed marriage. I expressed my regret that I was not able to make the marriage work between his mother and me. Once I confirmed his feelings, it was amazing how quickly his anger subsided. He immediately stopped crying and his demeanor and attitude changed. Although it was difficult not to react to him, I witnessed the miracle of grace and the power it has to heal a wounded child's heart. This experience continued to motivate me to let God define my circumstances instead of allowing my circumstances to define me.

DAY 35 COMING TO THE CROSS

My Dear Jesus,

What if I came to the foot of Your Cross with the knowledge that You just gave Your precious life for me? What if I had to witness You suffer on my behalf? How would it change me inside? What if it was I who took Your broken body from the Cross and held You in my arms with blood dripping from the many wounds You just suffered for me? Would I take this day any differently? Would I realize how much You love me by the sacrifice You just made for me, and love You more? What if it was I who cleaned Your lifeless body and gently wrapped it in a shroud, would I be more likely to tell those around me what You have done for me? What if it was I who cried outside Your tomb as they covered it with a boulder and shielded the opening from me so I could not reach out to You? Would I be able to feel the miracle of You in me more? What if it was I who held Your broken hands, divinely healed, and walked and talked with You as Your risen body revealed Your victory over the grave, would I serve Your kingdom more? Would I live each day with more joy in my heart knowing You are alive and with Your Father in Heaven? What if it was I who wrapped my arms around Your healed body and felt the power of Your love overcome me, as You left behind a light to guide me on this glorious journey together? Would I live a joyful life knowing that You are with me, and through You I can do all things? Lord with all the power of Your glorious Savior that lives within, help me live a joyful life radiating God's image to all I meet.

In Christ's glorious name, amen

DAY 36 WALKING HAND IN HAND WITH YOU

O Heavenly Father,

In my heart lives the presence of Jesus which has changed the way I experience the world. The awareness of my Lord and Savior living through me brings a peace and comfort to my day. Learning to bring all things to You in prayer has balanced my approach to all circumstances and given me hope and peace in my most difficult moments. Through the trials of life, my trust in You has grown as I have experienced a spiritual maturity and learned to praise You for all that life presents me. Growth through trials is a necessary part of building a kingdom of compassionate believers who can offer love to those who suffer only because they have suffered. I have learned to endure by relying on You and not the broken world around me. This has strengthened my relationship with You, Jesus, as we have walked hand in hand through these trials together. I am now ready to share a love and compassion with those in need of the Gospel of Christ that lives in me and through me. I am now changed, not by my own doing, but through the power and submission to Christ. With the knowledge that He has already conquered the world, I know there is nothing I cannot do or handle with His power leading the way.

In Christ's Holy name I pray, amen.

PHILIPPIANS 4:4-7 Rejoice in the Lord always. I will say it again: Rejoice! Let your gentleness be evident to all. The Lord is near. Do not be anxious about anything, but in every situation, by prayer and petition, with thanksgiving, present your requests to God. And the peace of God, which

> transcends all understanding, will guard your hearts and your minds in Christ Jesus.

I wrote this prayer when I was beginning to see and understand the transforming miracle of grace. Friends, clients, and co-workers started telling me how the grace I was showing toward my wife was affecting them. What they couldn't see was that the grace I was showing to her was the same grace I needed every day and which was literally transforming me from the inside out. I wanted so deeply to show those in my life God's reflection so that, when it was all said and done, I couldn't take any credit for what God had done. Even though we were not able to restore our marriage, we were able to rebuild a relationship that allows us to co-parent our son. It is a wonderful testament to the healing power of God's grace when my son's teacher, eight months into the school year, did not realize that we are divorced. We are always present together for him and keep in constant communication when events and issues come up at school or in life. We make the best effort to establish in two separate homes similar routines making it easier for our son to adjust. There are still many challenges, but when I see how well-adjusted my son is, I know it's entirely worth the effort.

DAY 37 KEEPING MY FOCUS ON YOU

O Heavenly Father,

You are the living water giving life to all who are thirsty. And I am thankful that my heart desires to be full of Your love and seeks Your wisdom in all things. Life is full of daily struggles consuming my thoughts and hampering me from focusing my life on serving You. Despite my lack of understanding of the day before me, You already know every trouble that lies hidden in the depths of my heart. Seeking first Your wisdom in all things will help me to establish a deeper and more complete understanding of life, keeping my focus off of self-centeredness and directing my thoughts toward You. Waking up and allowing You to be the center of my day depends on how much I am willing to trust You to handle my problems. Starting each day with a focused prayer keeps You in the driver's seat of my life.

O Heavenly Father,

I give my heart to You today so that Jesus can live through me. I give all the burdens of my heart to You and trust that You will handle them with a divine purpose to bring glory to You. I know I may not always understand the day before me, but I know there is a purpose to every day and I ask You to help me see the wisdom in all things. I know You are a good and loving God who desires to bring good out of all of my mistakes and the mistakes of others that affect my life. I am thankful that I continue to seek a greater understanding and a closer relationship with You. I ask You, Lord, with all the power you have granted Jesus, to open my heart to Your divine purpose for my life and help me to seek and understand Your divine wisdom in all things. I love You, Lord with all my heart, with all my soul and with all my strength.

In Christ's Holy name I pray, amen.

Luke 10:27 He answered, "Love the Lord your God with all your heart and with all your soul and with all your strength and with all your mind, and, Love your neighbor as yourself."

James 1:5 If any of you lacks wisdom, you should ask God, who gives generously to all without finding fault, and it will be given to you.

How easy is it to be distracted? Life seems to be traveling at such a pace that it is less about living and more about just keeping up. Often, looking for opportunities to serve God doesn't seem as important as completing my "to do" list. Before this trial hit me, life was about completing a long list of objectives. I thought there was a checklist of things I needed to complete in order for my life to have value and meaning. It definitely wasn't waking up each day and putting God's list of things to do first. That was on the back burner. "I'll get to that later, once I finish all my stuff." When life humbled me, I turned toward God, surrendered myself and prayed each day to follow His will. Life took on a whole new meaning when I dropped my "to do" list and started to seek God's will. God took care of all the things I worried about. My business is prospering; my son is thriving, happy, and well-adjusted; my financial situation has improved; and I am married to the woman God prepared for me. Now each day is about keeping my focus on God and taking it off myself. It's His "to do" list and I am here to complete what He has planned for me.

Keeping your focus on God to accomplish His plan is not an easy task, and I can say from my own personal experience pride will always creep in. I have had many setbacks, but now I have a plan that gets me back on track. It starts with getting to a quite place and simply asking God for direction. This is where I would challenge anyone who is skeptical. Try waking up every day, give thanks to God for the day ahead, put down your agenda, and ask God for direction. I think you will be amazed at how differently the day will look when you open your eyes to all the opportunities there are to serve God. Instead of being filled with anxiety about your tasks, you'll be filled with thankfulness every time you get a chance to serve God. I am not suggesting you neglect the things you have to do; I am only suggesting that they should not be the entire focus of your day. I am only encouraging you to keep your heart available to serve God instead of being too busy to look around for ways to help others in need. It's a matter of priority. At the end of the day I believe you'll be less stressed, less tired, and able to accomplish more with God driving than with you driving. The only real difference will be that the life you leave behind will be filled with God's accomplishments and not yours.

DAY 38 SEEING THE WORLD THROUGH YOUR EYES

O Heavenly Father,

I am being held in the arms of Jesus and I feel the warmth of His love covering me. Every day I am constantly reminded of how much You love me because the Gospel of Christ has opened my heart and shines through, healing my brokenness. Every step I take is stronger and more confident because I am beginning to let You lead the way. Seeing the world through Your eyes allows me to fall in love with You more every day as I realize what You have done for me. As I begin each day, Lord, I ask You for revelation and wisdom, revelation to know the truth and the wisdom to understand and walk in the likeness of my Lord and Savior. Every new day becomes another chance for me to show the world that Your Son is alive in me as I take all that comes my way with grace and thankfulness. Lord, I humbly ask You to allow the Love Story You created in me long ago to shine bright. As I give this day to You, Lord, help me use the power You have given the Holy Spirit to continue to transform me into the person You created me to be, so I may not fall short of bringing glory to You in all I say and all I do.

In Christ's name I pray, amen.

EPHESIANS 1:16-17 I have not stopped giving thanks for you, remembering you in my prayers. I keep asking that the God of our Lord Jesus Christ, the glorious Father, may give you the Spirit of wisdom and revelation, so that you may know him better.

DAY 39 YOUR LOVE IS MY LEGACY

O Heavenly Father,

I stand in awe of You. I am thankful that, through this journey, You have transformed my heart, not just to know You, but to feel Your presence that lies within me. Through pain and despair, You have opened doors to my heart, and revealed an overwhelming Love Story with Jesus that was not there before I began this journey.

Jesus, I am so in love with You, and I cannot imagine what each day will reveal to me as You continue to live through me. I know from this day forward every relationship I have will be more complete because I am able to look at them through Your eyes. Focusing on the constant Love Story with You has the power to change lives, heal broken hearts, move mountains, and cause the people around me to look inside themselves for the romance that lies within them. As you continue to romance my heart, You are calling on me to share this Love Story with everyone, including those who have caused me pain.

I can see, through Your divine wisdom, that pain brings a closeness to You that changes how I approach each day. Ultimately, joy and thanksgiving dominate my life because of the awareness of the miracle that You have given me to be my guide. Troubles then become opportunities to be closer to You, and the mistakes I make open my eyes to my dependency upon You. All aspects of life, even suffering, draw me closer to You, as I lay down my pride and give all of myself to You to heal the brokenness that's within me. As I continue this daily walk with You, my future is brighter and I can see with Your eyes the miracle of Your presence within me. I know the vast possibilities that exist as I begin each day with the words you have placed on my heart.

O Heavenly Father,

I give my heart to You today so that Jesus can guide my steps, lead my heart, and teach me constantly to follow Your divine path for my life. Although I may not understand the purpose of each day, I know You have already gone before me and prepared a way for me to bring glory to You. I trust, Lord, that You are my strength and my shield and you know that my purpose is not for my pleasure, but for Yours. So, as I begin this day in submission to You, I relinquish the burdens of my heart, so I can focus on Your purpose and Your will for my life.

It is my deepest understanding that I was not given the trials in my life so that I might tell my own story. Rather, the purpose was to show me the beauty of the Love Story You have given me in my Savior, so I might tell His story. I am no longer lost and truly found when the legacy I leave behind is Yours and not mine.

In Christ's glorious name I pray, amen.

Colossians 2:9-10 For in Christ all the fullness of the Deity lives in bodily form, and in Christ you have been brought to fullness. He is the head over every power and authority. Deuteronomy 6:5-7 Love the Lord your God with all your heart and with all your soul and with all your strength. These commandments that I give you today are to be on your hearts. Impress them on your children. Talk about them when you sit at home and when you walk along the road, when you lie down and when you get up.

2 Corinthians 4:15 All this is for your benefit, so that the grace that is reaching more and more people may cause thanksgiving to overflow to the glory of God.

Philippians 4:6 Do not be anxious about anything, but in every situation, by prayer and petition, with thanksgiving, present your requests to God.

Writing this prayer was emotional for me. I wrote it after church when one of our members stood in front of the congregation and gave his testimony. It was powerful as he explained how God transformed him and his family through a challenging trial. When he finished, our pastor mentioned that each seat in our sanctuary had a story to tell. When I arrived at home, I started thinking, "What would my story sound like?" One thought was clear to me; I had spent so much of my life trying to tell my story. So, I fell to my knees, lifted my hands to God and asked Him to help me tell His Story.

I guess the real question for me, "Did God put me here to tell His Story, or mine?" Our prideful self-serving soul wants to leave behind our legacy, the long list of accomplishments we achieve in our lifetime. I think most of my life that was my priority, building my resume. I guess from an ideological standpoint we can see it as working our way to heaven. The problem was I never asked God what I was supposed to be doing. It was my list. When God found me in the valley, I realized life wasn't about earning a ticket to heaven; it was about having a relationship with God. I have in recent years heard the statement, "It's not about religion, it's about relationship." The important part of this statement is, "What does it mean to have a relationship with God?" I have touched on this issue several times throughout this journal. I think it means setting time aside every day to spend with God, learning to listen to His Spirit guide you through the challenges of life. This is what strengthens your relationship with God, and builds the intimacy your soul desires. Deep within every soul is a desire to be connected to something or someone. It fundamentally completes us. This statement leads me back to my original question, "Did God put me here to tell His Story, or mine?"

Knowledge comes when we spend time trying to understanding our circumstances and growing through the challenges of life. This happens when we spend time with God reflecting, looking back at the choices we have made and how they have impacted our lives. Looking back on mine, I realized I allowed myself to be connected too deeply to a broken world. Putting my faith in people and things led me to sorrow when they were taken away. Emotionally, this really impacted me when it came to my son. Do I really want to leave him my legacy? What would that look like? I believe it would look like a broken mess. Yes, I have accomplished some good things in my life, but they don't add up to the legacy of my Savior. When I finally surrendered to the Holy Spirit and built an intimate bond with God, the curtains came down and I could see with clarity the purpose of the Cross. It was in that moment God touched me and my pride fell. Now my life was no longer about me or the broken legacy I would leave behind, it was about leaving a legacy for Christ. I want to show those in my life, especially my son, my Savior wasn't left hanging on a cross. He is alive and living through me. That is the real meaning of this prayer, asking God to help me leave behind His legacy and not mine. I want to make my life a picture He painted.

If you were painting a picture of your life, what would it look like? Would you paint bitterness, anger or resentment? I know God's picture for my life would look a lot different than the one I would paint for myself. The one he painted for humanity is found on the Cross and it is called grace. How important is it to God that we forgive? It is so important that He let His Son endure the Cross to free us from the burden of not being able to forgive. Do you think that Jesus suffered for you but not for those who have caused you pain? As hard as it is to imagine forgiving someone who has hurt you, it is the only way you can free yourself and not carry those wounds into your future. Letting go of yesterday's wounds allows God's grace and love to bring healing. Letting go makes the opportunities for tomorrow brighter. God knows the power of forgiveness and the freedom of letting go and this is one of the major reasons He gave up His Son. So we all can have a chance to let go of our past and move forward toward love.

Can you paint grace in your life? If so, what would grace look like to you?

As a result of my failed marriage, I can show the world what my Savior did for me and stop being the star in my story. It represents an opportunity for God to use my failure to paint the picture of His Son on my life.

DAY 40 THE MARRIAGE PRAYER

O Heavenly Father,

What is a marriage to You?

How can I make our marriage prosper?

The response:

My dear child, throughout your glorious life I have been preparing you to endure the wondrous trials of marriage. Marriage is something I created to add fulfillment to your lives. It is the joyful process of learning to lay aside one's life and, through submission to each other, become completely united to Me. I designed a man with all his strengths to live a full life serving me, but I left a part of him empty and incomplete. I designed a woman with all her strengths to live a full life serving me, but I also left a part of her empty and incomplete.

I designed marriage to bring two incomplete lives together and to unite them, bonding in each other's strengths and weaknesses. This is a wondrous process in which two incomplete souls unite themselves to Me, forming one complete body designed to strengthen each other's weaknesses and accentuating each other's strengths.

Marriage is one of the greatest gifts I have given to you. It allows a husband and wife to experience the intimate joy of loving each other through Me. It is the closest picture of Me you will share. The wisdom of this bond allows men and women to become one life designed to bring glory to Me. If I am the center of your love for each other, you will experience a life-long joy that is found in the presence of My Son I have printed on your hearts. This joy is called the Holy Spirit and it is how I speak My love to you. This gift is timeless. Marriage is the harmony of two separate lives bound together through sharing, giving, sacrificing, forgiving, and creating an intimate connection which brings out the greatest qualities I placed in each of you. This allows others to see My reflection in the love you share for each other. The more you put aside your selfishness for the betterment of your marriage, the more My love radiates outwardly from your marriage. This strengthens the bond between you both and draws you closer to Me.

Your marriage will prosper if you focus on what I have already given to you. It is the Love Story found in my beautiful son Jesus. Every lesson about love is found in His wisdom printed on your hearts. If you make Him the center of your relationship, you are guaranteed prosperity. In Him lie the secrets of love. It is a never-ending, all-enduring romance that is built around grace. Allowing each other to stumble while continuing to love is the real secret to a life-long partnership. I ask only that you offer the same grace to your spouse that I have given you in My glorious Son Jesus.

Finally, remember that spending intimate time with Me allows Me the chance to reveal things that I desire for you to improve. You must bring all your problems before Me. I will heal, mend, and nurture your marriage and watch you both grow closer to Me.

1 Corinthians 13:4-13 Love is patient, love is kind. It does not envy, it does not boast, it is not proud. It does not dishonor others, it is not self-seeking, it is not easily angered, it keeps no record of wrongs. Love does not delight in evil but rejoices with the truth. It always protects, always trusts, always hopes, always perseveres.

> Love never fails. But where there are prophecies, they will cease; where there are tongues, they will be stilled; where there is knowledge, it will pass away. For we know in part and we prophesy in part, but when completeness comes, what is in part disappears. When I was a child, I talked like a child, I thought like a child, I reasoned like a child. When I became a man, I put the ways of childhood behind me. For now we see only a reflection as in a mirror; then we shall see face to face. Now I know in part; then I shall know fully, even as I am fully known. And now these three remain: faith, hope and love. But the greatest of these is love.

The Marriage Prayer is a prayer I wrote as God directed my heart toward His. It accurately describes everything that was missing in my failed marriage, and gave me an outline to follow in my current marriage. I am now truly happy in my marriage not because my life is absent of trials, but because I am now dependent on God to carry me, my wife, and my son down the beautiful road called life. I know now it won't be easy, but it will be worth it.

13 Conclusion

I found it challenging to write a conclusion to this book because God's work in me isn't finished. I know He has so much more planned for my life. When I began writing, I wasn't writing a book, I was just trying to connect to God, trying to heal. Yet the instant I felt Him touch me, I was blindsided by His love and began building my relationship with Him through the Holy Spirit. Despite the tears I shed, the intimacy I experienced when I openly shared myself with Him gave me a whole new purpose to my trial. It helped me understand how my pride stood in the way of experiencing God and gave me a better understanding of my limitations. Humility helped me build a relationship with God as my dependency on Him grew each day. Even when my heart ached to the point I felt empty and breathless, He offered me a peace nothing else has ever filled. Reflecting back and looking forward, I learned the purpose of life is to be closer to God. There is no greater purpose for which we are made. The closer we are to God the more we can see and experience the world from His perspective. Herein lies the secret to a happy life and it is called grace. If each of us can find what we have already been given through the power of the Holy Spirit, we too will experience the glory of grace. The healing power of God's love will flow through our lives into this broken world.

This maybe difficult to understand if you have never experienced a point in your life where you felt defeated, a moment when you acknowledged that life has won, and you reach out to God and surrender your pride. That is when the blinders fall and God reveals His Love Story. When you experience this moment, your trial has led you to the foot of the Cross. Looking up you'll see the Love Story for which you were made and the love it took to free you from the burdens you maybe carrying now: anger, loss, bitterness, resentment, and an unwillingness to forgive. Close your eyes and picture yourself standing at the foot of the Cross. What do you think Jesus would say to help you?

Could you imagine what tomorrow would be like if your only purpose was to wake up and serve God and connect to His Love Story? What would your day look like if you chose to breathe new life into all situations?

Remember that your life is a story being written, and you have a choice to let the Spirit of God help you write it or rely on yourself alone. I believe that if you choose to let God write your story, the ending you'll be writing will be filled with more joy than you can imagine.

One of my favorite song lyrics comes from *Just Be Held* by Casting Crowns. It says: "My life's not fallen apart, it's fallen into place." I pray this journal has opened your heart to God's Love Story and through your surrender you have experienced what it feels like to be blindsided by the healing power of the Holy Spirit. I pray God's love has washed away the burdens that have held you captive and has given you hope for tomorrow. May the picture God paints for your life be as beautiful as the one He has painted for mine.

The following Scriptures guided this journey:

All scripture in this journal is quoted from the New International Version (NIV)

MATTHEW 4:1-11 Then Jesus was led by the Spirit into the wilderness to be tempted by the devil. After fasting forty days and forty nights, he was hungry. The tempter came to him and said, "If you are the Son of God, tell these stones to become bread."

Jesus answered, "It is written: 'Man shall not live on bread alone, but on every word that comes from the mouth of God.'"

Then the devil took him to the holy city and had him stand on the highest point of the temple. "If you are the Son of God," he said, "throw yourself down. For it is written: "'He will command his angels concerning you, and they will lift you up in their hands, so that you will not strike your foot against a stone.

Jesus answered him, "It is also written: 'Do not put the Lord your God to the test.'"

Again, the devil took him to a very high mountain and showed him all the kingdoms of the world and their splendor. "All this I will give you," he said, "if you will bow down and worship me."

Jesus said to him, "Away from me, Satan! For it is written: 'Worship the Lord your God, and serve him only.'"

Then the devil left him, and angels came and attended him.

Exodus 15:25-26 Then Moses cried out to the LORD, and the LORD showed him a piece of wood. He threw it into the water, and the water became fit to drink. There the LORD issued a ruling and instruction for them and put them to the test. He said..."If you listen carefully to the LORD your God and do what is right in his eyes, if you pay attention to his commands and keep all his decrees, I will not bring on you any of the diseases I brought on the Egyptians, for I am the LORD, who heals you."

James 1:2-5 Consider it pure joy, my brothers and sisters, whenever you face trials of many kinds, because you know that the testing of your faith produces perseverance. Let perseverance finish its work so that you may be mature and complete, not lacking anything. If any of you lacks wisdom, you should ask God, who gives generously to all without finding fault, and it will be given to you.

1 Thessalonians 5:15-18 Make sure that nobody pays back wrong for wrong, but always strive to do what is good for each other and for everyone else. Rejoice always, pray continually, give thanks in all circumstances; for this is God's will for you in Christ Jesus.

Mark 11:25 And when you stand praying, if you hold anything against anyone, forgive him, so that your Father in heaven may forgive you your sins.

2 CORINTHIANS 5:17-18 Therefore, if anyone is in Christ, the new creation has come: The old has gone, the new is here! All this is from God, who reconciled us to himself through Christ and gave us the ministry of reconciliation...